T0340934

# THE RUSSIAN FAR EAST

## Strategic Priorities for
## Sustainable Development

# THE RUSSIAN FAR EAST

## Strategic Priorities for Sustainable Development

Sergey Darkin and Vladimir Kvint

*New York*

**Under the research supervision of
Dr. Sergey Darkin and Dr. Vladimir Kvint.**


*The Pacific Investment Group*

*Lomonosov Moscow State University's Center for Strategic Studies
at the Institute of Mathematical Studies of Complex Systems*

*"AksionBKG" LLC*

| Apple Academic Press Inc. | Apple Academic Press Inc. |
| 3333 Mistwell Crescent | 9 Spinnaker Way |
| Oakville, ON L6L 0A2 | Waretown, NJ 08758 |
| Canada | USA |

©2017 by Apple Academic Press, Inc.
*Exclusive worldwide distribution by CRC Press, a member of Taylor & Francis Group*
No claim to original U.S. Government works
Printed in the United States of America on acid-free paper
International Standard Book Number-13: 978-1-77188-433-4 (print)
International Standard Book Number-13: 978-1-77188-434-1 (ebook)

---

### Library and Archives Canada Cataloguing in Publication

---

Darkin, Sergey, author
The Russian Far East : strategic priorities for sustainable development/Sergey Darkin and Vladimir Kvint.
Includes bibliographical references and index.
ISBN 978-1-77188-433-4 (hardcover)

1. Sustainable development--Russia (Federation)--Russian Far East.
2. Russian Far East (Russia)--Economic conditions--21st century. 3. Russian
Far East (Russia)--Strategic aspects. I. Kvint, V. L. (Vladimir L'vovich), author II. Title.

HC340.12.Z7F27 2016        330.957'7        C2016-901694-3

---

### Library of Congress Cataloging-in-Publication Data

Names: Darkin, S. M. (Sergeæi Mikhaæilovich), 1963- author. | Kvint, V. L. (Vladimir L'vovich), author.
Title: The Russian Far East : strategic priorities for sustainable development / Sergey Darkin and Vladimir Kvint.
Description: 1st ed. | New Jersey : Apple Academic Press, 2016. | Includes bibliographical references and index.
Identifiers: LCCN 2016011012| ISBN 9781771884334 (hardcover : alk. paper) | ISBN 9781771884334 (eBook)
Subjects: LCSH: Sustainable development--Russia (Federation)--Russian Far East. | Russian Far East (Russia)--Economic conditions--21st century. | Russian Far East (Russia)--Strategic aspects.
Classification: LCC HC340.12.Z7 F27754623 2016b | DDC 338.957/7--dc23
LC record available at https://lccn.loc.gov/2016011012

---

Apple Academic Press also publishes its books in a variety of electronic formats. Some content that appears in print may not be available in electronic format. For information about Apple Academic Press products, visit our website at **www.appleacademicpress.com** and the CRC Press website at **www.crcpress.com**

# CONTENTS

# ABOUT THE AUTHORS

**Sergey Darkin,** PhD, was the Governor of the Primorsky Region of the Russian Federation from 2001 to 2012, Deputy Minister of Regional Development of the Russian Federation from 2012 to 2014, and is currently President of the Pacific Investment Group (TIGR) since 2014. Dr. Darkin currently serves as a board member of several leading companies and banks. He is an authority in issues of Asia-Pacific economic development, and a well-established professional in regional cooperation and the shipping and fishing industries, among other areas.

**Vladimir Kvint,** PhD, has been a professor of strategy, management systems and international economics at Fordham University, New York University's Stern School of Business, American and LaSalle Universities, and Babson College and serves as chair of the Financial Strategy Department in the Moscow School of Economics at Moscow State University. He is also Research Director at the Center for Strategic Studies at the Institute of Complex Systems Mathematical Research (CSS ICSMR). Dr. Kvint is a member of the Bretton Woods Committee, a lifetime foreign member of the Russian Academy of Sciences, a U.S. Fulbright Scholar, and a well-established strategic advisor.

## Other Contributors

M. Alimuradov, PhD
A. Karpov
R. Kapinos
A. Korbukh, PhD
I. Tushkanov, PhD
D. Ugolkov, PhD
I. Malenkov
A. Fedyaev

# ACKNOWLEDGMENTS

---

For assistance in the preparation of this Study, the authors are grateful to the Plenipotentiary of the President of the Russian Federation in the Far Eastern Federal District, Deputy Prime Minister of the Russian Federation, **Yury Trutnev**. The authors are very thankful for the help of Elizabeth Schmermund in translating this book.

# KEY DEFINITIONS

*Cluster* – an interrelated group of organizations (companies, organizations, universities, banks, etc.) concentrated in a certain area that includes: the suppliers of products, components, and specialized services; infrastructure; research institutes; universities; and other organizations that complement each other and reinforce the competitive advantages of individual companies and of the cluster as a whole.

*Strategic competitive advantage* – main factors determining strategic success in a certain industry, region, or other entity.

*National interests* – the most important strategic needs of a particular country, consciously formulated at the highest level of its government.

*A project of strategic priority development* – a separate entity or its subdivision, the development of which will improve a country or entity's competitiveness on world markets, as well as the development of related industries, science, and social spheres.

*Strategy* – the search, formulation, and doctrine-developing system, which will provide long-term success if followed faithfully and fully implemented. Strategy is the result of the systematic environmental analysis and existing projections of future conditions on the basis of strategic thinking, deep knowledge, and intuition. The final product of this analysis is a formalized strategy, combining the updated forecast, mission, vision, priorities, and long-term goals and objectives with a detailed scenario, and requiring the implementation of all elements of the strategic management system abiding with the law.

*Strategic priorities* – factors and wide objectives (economic, social, technological, natural, among others) that primarily determine the successful development and implementation of the strategy.

***A territory with advanced social and economic development*** – a territory (in the Russian Pacific Coast region) where, in accordance with the government's decision to develop the region, special legal regimes for infrastructure development, businesses, and other activities have been established.[1]

***Territories of priority development*** – territories that are adjacent to priority development projects and share a common infrastructure with these projects, where industrial or technological parks and start-up companies may be allocated. These parks being designated for:

- introducing technologies already used in manufacturing in other industries' projects of priority development;
- carrying out innovations in order to widely implement them during the production of priority development for the formation of additional strategic competitive advantages.

---

[1] "Territories with advanced social and economic development and other government support in the Far East" Federal Law draft (prepared by Ministry of Economic Development of the Russian Federation).

# LIST OF ABBREVIATIONS

| | |
|---|---|
| AIC | Agro-Industrial Complex |
| CES | Common Economic Space |
| EAEU | Eurasian Economic Union |
| ES | Electrical Substation |
| EU | European Union |
| CHPP | Coal Handling Processing Plant |
| DIR | Defense Industry of Russia |
| FTIP | Federal Target Investment Program |
| FTP | Federal Target Program |
| FEFD | Far Eastern Federal District |
| FNPS | Floating Nuclear Power Station |
| HPP | Hydropower Plant |
| Implementer | LLC AksionBKG |
| JSC | Joint-Stock Company |
| LNG | Liquefied Natural Gas |
| LCC | Contract Life Cycle |
| MEDRF | Ministry of Economic Development of the Russian Federation |
| MET | Mineral Exemption Tax |
| NSR | Northern Sea Route |
| OPS | Oil Pumping Station |
| PC | Public Company |
| PR | Pacific Rim (Asia-Pacific region) |
| REPS | Renewable energy power station |
| SC | State Corporation |
| SEA | Southeast Asia |
| SEZ | Special Economic Zone |
| TAD | Territory of the Advanced (Social and Economic) Development |

| TPCS | Thermal Power Central Station |
| TPP | Thermal Power Plant |
| TPS | Thermal Power Station |
| UES of the East | United Energy System of the Pacific Coast Region |

# INTRODUCTION:
# THE STRATEGIC VISION

The Russian Pacific Coast region[2] is one of the most strategically important regions of Russia and its development carries nationwide and global significance. The Russian Pacific Coast region and the development of its manufacturing strength determine Russia's role in a major economic area of the world: the Asia-Pacific region. The degree to which the transportation, telecommunications, and social infrastructure of the Pacific Coast of Russia are developed will strategically predetermine the export potential of the country and the future of the global economy.

Due to the pure theoretical absence of competition in the northeastern part of the Pacific Ocean during the entire post-Soviet period, Russia did not develop strategy and implement large-scale economic programs for the development of port facilities in the waters of the Chukchi Sea, Bering Sea, the Sea of Okhotsk, and the Sea of Japan. The infrastructure connecting the ports of the Baikal-Amur Mainline with the Trans-Siberian Railway is, for the most part, "stuck" in the 1980s.

The issue of developing Russian strategic potential in the Asia-Pacific region is complicated by an almost total suspension of commercial and fishing shipbuilding. Unfortunately, the resources allocated to the Russian Pacific Coast region, in these times of raging deficit, do not concentrate on Russian national priorities in the Far Eastern Federal District. This research report presents the strategic scenario for the most effective long-term use of these resources.

Pursuant to the situation explained above, the objective of this study is to determine the main strategic competitive advantages in accordance with Russia's strategic priorities in the Russian Pacific Coast region in order to maximize the country's strategic competitiveness in the global market and, especially, in the Asia-Pacific region. These strategic competitive advantages are determined based on the geopolitical position of

---

[2] Please note that throughout this text the "Russian Pacific Coast region" and the "Russian Far East" are synonymous.

the Federal District and on the presence of natural resources within the District's territory, as seen below. The following industries have strategic competitive advantages on a global scale.

1. Geopolitical strategic advantages:
   - Access to the world's oceans and the Arctic;
   - The lengthy ocean coastline;
   - Proximity to the countries of the Asia-Pacific region;
   - Location on transcontinental vectors and regional trade routes;
   - The common border with China.
2. Strategically competitive natural resources:
   - Minerals, such as:
     i. Coal (large reserves, open pit method);
     ii. Gas and oil (the world's largest oil and gas production projects);
     iii. Iron ore (high quality elements);
     iv. Uranium ore (the world's largest deposit);
     v. Gold (44% of all Russian natural gold reserves);
     vi. Diamonds (more than 25% of the world's production);
     vii. Tin (13% of all Russian natural tin reserves);
     viii. Lead (12% of all Russian natural lead reserves);
     ix. Graphite (the largest deposit in Russia);
     x. Rare earth metals (deposits exceed the rest of the world's total reserves);
     xi. Fresh water (the largest reserves of natural fresh water containing silver);
     xii. Forest resources (27% of all Russian wood resources);
     xiii. Ocean bio-resources (70% of all Russian production of fish and seafood).
3. Strategically competitive sectors of the economy:
   - Oil and gas industry;
   - Coal industry;
   - Mining industry;
   - Chemical industry;
   - Logging economy;
   - Engineering;

- Transportation and logistics;
- Fishing industry;
- Reindeer and sea mammal hunting.

More than 60 high strategic priority investment projects are outlined in this report. Successful implementation of these investment projects will achieve the following results:

- Improvement of Russia's strategic competitiveness on the global marketplace;
- Optimization of financial, material and labor resources by concentrating them on these prioritized strategic projects;
- Development of adjacent production projects in industrial clusters around the prioritized facilities, also known as "the multiplier effect," to save limited resources and maximize effect;
- Diversification of the regional economy for the sustainable economic development of the country.

In the future, the results of this strategic study should be used for resource optimization through economic-mathematical modeling methods.

*Sergey Darkin*
*Vladimir Kvint*
2015

# CHAPTER 1

# STRATEGIC APPROACH TO THE STUDY OF REGIONAL PROSPECTS: THE SELECTION OF DEVELOPMENT PRIORITIES IN THE MACRO-REGIONS OF THE RUSSIAN FEDERATION IN THE NEXT 10 YEARS

The strategic approach in determining development prospects in these regions makes it possible to efficiently concentrate resources on the most promising and competitive development priorities. One of the most significant limitations of any strategy is the impossibility of implementing potentially profitable projects for a limited time in certain areas due to the limitation of necessary economic factors.

This is why the development of basic economic factors in regions must be the basis for the successful implementation of strategic projects. Without forming competitive advantages in the economy, the achievement of significantly sustainable social effects will not be possible. When beginning to develop strategic documents, the emphasis should be placed on economic performance, by changing the nature of documents from "socio-economic" to "economic and social." This formulation of the problem enables the best use of existing economic potential to achieve long-term development goals. Meanwhile, the solution of social problems should be based on economic achievements and be a logical result of the successful implementation of the strategy, and not its precondition. Strategic priorities for the country, regions, individual enterprises, and manufacturers should be formed by considering the feasibility of their implementation in the medium-term strategy development period. Priority areas strategy proposes the usage of a limited set of resources.

First of all, it is important to assess the sufficiency and availability of the necessary resources. In the industrial sector, the development of which requires real investments, the cost of production, and respectably, the projected earnings and profitability are largely dependent on a number of factors. Among them is the presence of the required number of high-quality raw materials, the cost of production, development, and delivery to the place of production that satisfies the conditions of manufacturing. This creates relatively competitive advantages for potential investors. Therefore, the first criterion in selecting strategic development priorities for the macro regions of Russia should be the availability of resources, the usage of which are supported economically.

The effective development of manufacturing and the implementation of strategically important investment projects are not possible without a sufficient, qualified, and experienced workforce. Without providing industry with both highly productive human resources and modern manufacturing methods, you cannot run investment processes and efficient operations even with available natural resources. In the end, a lack of human resources could lead to available natural resources not being included in the economic turnover and staying "frozen" for a long period, which, additionally, could lead to missed competitive advantages. The security of Russian labor supply is an acute problem for the domestic economy and can be explained not only by the shortage in the working-age population, but also by its uneven distribution among regions. For example, the eastern regions of Russia, with colossal amounts of natural resources and proven reserves of various minerals, are the least populated. The low population of these regions and the high population concentration around several major cities severely limit the implementation of potentially profitable investment projects. Therefore, the next selection criterion of the strategic priorities of the region's development is the availability of the necessary manpower with the required qualifications. In certain cases, it is possible to quickly resolve the lack of labor force, especially when the need for production workers arises. However, to develop potential engineering professionals, as well as qualified managers, significant financial and time expenditures might be required. One of the reasons Russian strategic documents are not often implemented is not a lack of natural resources, but the inability to train professionals in the stipulated time.

The successful implementation of investment projects depends not only on available natural and labor resources, but also on the availability of production capacity and industrial infrastructure. An important requirement for potential investors is the availability to implement an investment process on the basis of the production capacity already accumulated in the region's economic system. Their inclusion in the operation of new projects significantly reduces the cost to fixed capital, and modernization and reconstruction requires considerably smaller amounts to be taken from the current turnover than forming a material and technical base from scratch. The presence of infrastructure provides convenient access to major highways, energy networks, and markets. Some projects, however large, cannot provide effectively if it is necessary to first develop transportation or production infrastructure. The region that is planned to have priority development in certain industries must be ready to receive investments. In this case, given the lack of infrastructure, it is possible to construct such objects on the basis of public–private partnerships with the re-assignment of the burden of their construction and operation between participants.

In the process of implementing strategic investment, one of the most important objectives is the ensured supply of modern high-performance equipment to manufacturers. In a resource-poor setting, technological processes with high levels of automation can ensure the production process' stability and the satisfactory generation of profits for investors. This is why the next criterion when selecting development priority should be the availability of necessary equipment and the availability of adequate funds to finance its acquisition. In addition, it is necessary to take into account a company's ability to generate a sufficient money supply to provide functioning productions with current assets.

Modern industries work under the increasing influence of the "knowledge" economy. To insure a high level of competitiveness, it is necessary to introduce modern scientific technology. That is why it is crucial not to be limited only to findings of domestic research, but to learn from accumulated global scientific and technological knowledge. Therefore, the next criterion when selecting development priority should be the availability of or the accessibility to modern scientific and technological achievements.

With the current sharp weakening of the Ruble, one of the basic criteria for the selection of investment projects that have high development potential is the selection of projects with a high proportion of exports. Thus, the export potential of the enterprises located in the region would be used as efficiently as possible.

The scarcity of resources always assumes their concentration in vital priorities, the inadequate maintenance and development of which leads to irreversible threats. Therefore, in the coming years Russia's regions should focus on the extraordinary concentration of resources in a narrow range of priority areas. Previously developed regional and domestic economy industries and individual large-scale production strategies should be re-examined and, if necessary, revised in terms of the implementation of Russia's vital interests. Meanwhile, the Russian Federation's advancement strategy can only be developed and effectively implemented when all policies of the Federal districts and regions of Russia, industries, and vital individual enterprises focus rigidly on a limited number of selective priorities to implement this highlighted principle. Thus, the following categories for prioritizing should be allocated to the Far Eastern Federal District in general and the regions of the district in particular:

## 1.1. FIRST-DEGREE PRIORITIES

Russia's global competitive advantages localized in the Far Eastern Federal District and its regions:

- Competitive advantages where Russia keeps and should maintain its global leadership.
- Competitive advantages where Russia is still behind among competitors on the global arena, but where this situation can be resolved, and Russia's leadership can be restored.
- Competitive advantages that were revealed or formed only recently in the Far Eastern Federal District, and could be used as platforms

for initial investments, which would provide Russia with strategic leadership in fundamentally new areas.

# 1.2. SECOND-DEGREE PRIORITIES

These priorities provide internal social stability in Russia on the basis of using the domestic competitive advantages of the Far Eastern Federal District and federal regions located within its boundaries:

- The support and development of infrastructure that ensures food security in Russia.
- The support and development of infrastructure that strengthens and supports the health of the Russian population. This includes strengthening and developing residential areas, which, in current conditions, is possible only at the level of first- and second-degree priorities implementation.
- The support and development of infrastructure that aids population growth in areas of Russia's national interests in the Far Eastern Federal District.
- The support, strengthening, and rapid development of educational and scientific potential in Russia via strengthening the current and limited construction of new educational and research centers in strategic Federal districts and regions of the Federation.
- The support and strengthening of Russian military potential in strategic Federal districts and regions of the Federation.

Other degrees of priorities should not be included in the strategy of conserving, strengthening, and developing Russia's vitally important priorities on the basis of its competitive advantages. An exception may only be made with priorities and independent strategic centers whose support of effective working conditions would guarantee the implementation of first- and second-degree priorities. Using the highest development strategy for the medium-term strategic perspective allows, even under high scarcity of resources, the achievement and implementation of the country's orientations and approved priorities proposed by the political leadership.

The concentration of main resources in completing first- and second-degree priorities does not cancel the current plans and programs that are being implemented in the country. It only highlights the high priority of these priorities in resource-poor settings.

# CHAPTER 2

# STRATEGIES, PLANS, AND PROGRAMS FOR THE ECONOMIC-SOCIAL DEVELOPMENT OF THE FAR EASTERN FEDERAL DISTRICT OF THE RUSSIAN FEDERATION AND ITS REGIONS

## 2.1. THE FAR EASTERN FEDERAL DISTRICT

### 2.1.1. THE STRATEGY

Strategy for the Socio-Economic Development of the Far East and the Baikal Region through 2025 approved by the Instruction of the Government of the Russian Federation N 2094-p. Dated 28.12.2009.

**Priorities:**

- Improving the region's competitiveness.

**Goals:**

- Creating conditions for developing an advanced economic specialization profile of Russian regions located in the Far East and Baikal Region based on natural resources; industrial, human, and scientific potential within federal and sectoral development strategies; and socio-economic development strategies of the Russian Federation's regions and municipalities, as well as strategic programs of large companies;

- Forming a stable settlement system based on regional areas of advancing economic growth with a comfortable social environment;
- Removing barriers to economic and social integration for the Far East and Baikal Region to the rest of Russia and increasing the competitiveness of products, goods, and services in accordance with their economic specialization profiles through the formation of a regulatory legal framework that defines specific conditions for pricing, tariff, customs, tax, and fiscal policies;
- Forming the population and labor force to the extent required by the economic challenges the region is facing and improving the quality of human resources;
- Preserving and supporting the traditional lifestyles of the Russian Federation's indigenous minorities (hereinafter referred to as "the Northern minorities").

## 2.1.2. ACTION PLANS

The strategy for implementation of the plan includes actions that are aimed at the creation of conditions for the effective development of the region's economy (1).

## 2.1.3. STATE PROGRAMS

The federal purpose-oriented program "Social and Economic Development of the Far East and Baikal region through 2025" (2).

## 2.2. THE SAKHA (YAKUTIA) REPUBLIC

## 2.2.1. THE STRATEGY

A complex scheme for the development of production forces, as well as transportation and energy industries, in the Sakha (Yakutia) Republic through 2020.

**Priorities:**

- Diversifying the economy;
- Developing the regional energy sector.

**Goals:**

- Creating the transportation, energy, and information infrastructure;
- Developing the construction industry;
- Improving the spatial organization of the economy;
- Ensuring sustainable development for the unique regional ecosystems.

## 2.2.2. ACTION PLANS

Set of measures for the implementation of main provisions of the scheme, including:

- Developing the transportation network;
- Developing the oil and gas industry;
- Developing the electric power industry;
- Further developing the coal industry;
- Creating oil, gas, and coal-chemical processing industries.

## 2.2.3. STATE PROGRAMS

State programs in the Sakha (Yakutia) Republic are listed in Table 2.1.

**TABLE 2.1.**   List of State Programs in the Sakha (Yakutia) Republic

| Number | Name of the state program |
|--------|---------------------------|
| 1 | "Development of the health system in the Sakha (Yakutia) Republic for the period from 2012 through 2016" |
| 2 | "Development of the education system in the Sakha (Yakutia) Republic for the period from 2012 through 2016" |
| 3 | "Development of the professional education system in the Sakha (Yakutia) Republic for the period from 2012 through 2016" |
| 4 | "Development of the social security system in the Sakha (Yakutia) Republic for the period from 2012 through 2017" |

**TABLE 2.1.** (Continued).

| Number | Name of the state program |
|--------|---------------------------|
| 5 | "Employment assistance program in the Sakha (Yakutia) Republic for the period from 2012 through 2017" |
| 6 | "Housing program in the Sakha (Yakutia) Republic for the period from 2012 through 2017" |
| 7 | "Development of the electricity system and utilities services in the Sakha (Yakutia) Republic for the period from 2012 through 2017" |
| 8 | "Prevention of crime and maintenance of public order for the period from 2012 through 2016" |
| 9 | "The anti-narcotics policy implementation in the Sakha (Yakutia) Republic for the period from 2012 through 2017" |
| 10 | "Population's life safety in the Sakha (Yakutia) Republic for the period from 2012 through 2017" |
| 11 | "Implementation of family, population and youth policies in the Sakha (Yakutia) Republic for the period from 2012 through 2016" |
| 12 | "Development of sports culture and physical education in the Sakha (Yakutia) Republic for the period from 2012 through 2016" |
| 13 | "Creating necessary conditions for the cultural development of the indigenous people of Yakutia for the period from 2012 through 2017" |
| 14 | "Development of the regional mass media for the period from 2012 through 2017" |
| 15 | "Promoting harmony in relations between different ethnicities in the Sakha (Yakutia) Republic for the period from 2012 through 2016" |
| 16 | "Environment protection in the Sakha (Yakutia) Republic for the period from 2012 through 2017" |
| 17 | "Development of the water-economic system of the Sakha (Yakutia) Republic for the period from 2012 through 2017" |
| 18 | "Hunting resources preservation for the period from 2012 through 2017" |
| 19 | "Development of forestry for the period from 2012 through 2016" |
| 20 | "Development of the living facilities, major building objects and life-support systems in seismic zones in the Sakha (Yakutia) Republic for the period from 2012 through 2017" |
| 21 | "Development of innovation and science in the Sakha (Yakutia) Republic for the period from 2012 through 2017" |
| 22 | "Development of entrepreneurship in the Sakha (Yakutia) Republic for the period from 2012 through 2017" |
| 23 | "Development of tourism (including inner tourism) on the territory of the Sakha (Yakutia) Republic for the period from 2012 through 2017" |

**TABLE 2.1.** (Continued).

| Number | Name of the state program |
|--------|---------------------------|
| 24 | "Development of agriculture, including agriculture regulations for the period from 2012 through 2020" |
| 25 | "Gasification of human settlements and ensuring for gas supply reliability in the Sakha (Yakutia) Republic for the period from 2012 through 2016" |
| 26 | "Geological survey on the territory of the Sakha (Yakutia) Republic for the period from 2012 through 2017" |
| 27 | "Development of the transportation system of the Sakha (Yakutia) Republic for the period from 2012 through 2017" |
| 28 | "Development of the information society in the Sakha (Yakutia) Republic for the period from 2012 through 2016" |
| 29 | "Energy-effective economy for the period from 2012 through 2016 and for the period until 2020" |
| 30 | "Development of HR potential of the Sakha (Yakutia) Republic for the period from 2012 through 2017" |
| 31 | "Property management for the period from 2012 through 2017" |
| 32 | "Regional economic policy for the period from 2012 through 2017" |
| 33 | "State finance and government debt management or the period from 2012 through 2017" |
| 34 | "International cooperation and foreign economic activity of the Sakha (Yakutia) Republic for the period from 2012 through 2017" |
| 35 | "Improving mobilization preparedness for the period from 2012 through 2017" |

## 2.2.4. PROJECTS LISTED IN STRATEGIES AND STATE PROGRAMS

Projects listed in the "Scheme of the complex development of the Sakha (Yakutia) Republic":

- Development of iron ore deposits in South Yakutia;
- Construction of a steel plant on the basis of iron ore deposits in South Yakutia;
- Development of the Sardana lead-zinc deposit;
- Development of the Mir underground mine;
- Deep horizons mining of the Udachnaya tube;

- Development of the Aihal underground mine;
- Gold mining in the Nizhneyakokitskoye ore deposit;
- Development of the Kyuchus gold deposit;
- Mobile ore-dressing plant (MODP);
- Construction of the gold mining complex at the Kuranakh ore field;
- Development of the Nezhdaninskoye deposit;
- Development of the Tomtor niobium in the rare-earth deposit;
- Development of the Prognoz deposit (Verkhoyansk District);
- Development of Elkon District uranium deposits and construction of mining and steel plants;
- Organization of light sections mini-steel production (Yakutsk);
- Further development of the gold and antimony deposit in Sentachanskii and organization of the steel plant for production of antimony trioxide by LLC Zvezda in Ust-Nera;
- Desovskoye iron ore deposit (South Yakutia);
- Construction of the underground mine ALROSA JSC;
- Modernization of the Neryungri coal mine;
- Construction of the Chulmakansky mine;
- Construction of the Denisovskaya mine;
- Construction of the Kholodnikanskaya mine;
- Construction of the Inaglinskaya mine;
- Construction of the Lokuchakitskaya mine;
- Development of the Kyuchusskiy gold deposit (Ust-Yansky District);
- Increase in gold production at Kuranakh ore field (Aldan district);
- Development of the Seligdarsky apatite deposits (Aldan district);
- Pipeline from Eastern Siberia to the Pacific Ocean;
- Implementation of the Vostok-50 project in the territory of the Sakha (Yakutia) Republic taking into account the Chayandinskoye deposit (according to Gazprom JSC's latest program);
- Construction of the Yakutsk-Magadan railway line (including development of feasibility study and design estimate documentation);
- Construction of the Ust-Kut – Nepa – Lensk railway line (including development of the FS and DED);
- Construction of the Khani – Olekminsk railway line (including development of the FS and DED);

- Construction, modernization, and renovation of cargo and passenger coasters;
- Renovation, upgrading, and repairing of the water transportation infrastructure;
- Amga road (Yakutsk – Amga – Ust-Maya – Eldikan – Yugorenok – Ayan);
- Kobyai road (Asyma – Byas-Kyuel – Kobyai – Sangar);
- Umnas road (Yakutsk – Pokrovsk – Olekminsk – Daban – Chapaevo – Turukta – Lensk);
- Yana road (Topolinoe – Batagai – Ust-Kuiga – Deputatskiy – Belaya gora);
- Yakutsk Airport development activities;
- Modernization of air traffic control systems;
- Development of oil and gas deposits in: Talakansky, Srednebotuobinsky, Taas Yuryahsky, Verkhnevilyuchanskoye, Srednetyungskoye;
- Development of the Chayandinskoye oil and gas deposit;
- Production of synthetic motor fuels from the natural gas in Yakutsk;
- Development of the Elga coal deposit;
- Construction of a nuclear power station (floating nuclear power station) with a lead-cooled fast reactor – 10–40 MWe plants;
- Creation of a gas chemical complex (GCC) in the Yakutsk site for electricity generation from the oil-associated gas;
- Construction of the Yakutsk gas chemical and gas processing complex;
- Construction of the Irelyakhneft oil refinery in Mirny district;
- Construction of an ethylene factory in Neryungri;
- Completion of the Berkakit – Tommot – Yakutsk railway line with the combined rail and road bridge on the Lena river in Yakutsk;
- Completion of the Ulak – Elga railway line leading to the coal deposit;
- Fitting the inland navigation transportation system with new "river-sea" vessels;
- Construction of dry cargo vessels series for the development of Elga and Neryungri deposits of export coals;
- Reconstruction and overall repairs of the Lena federal highway to comply with III category standards;

- Completion of the construction and reconstruction of Kolyma federal highway;
- Completion of the construction and reconstruction of Viluy road;
- Ust-Kut-Vitim-Lensk road;
- Tommot-Belkachi Ust-Mil road;
- Construction of a new Lena – Olekminsk – Aldan road;
- Construction of a gypsum processing factory in the city of Olekminsk;
- Construction of a brick factory in the city of Yakutsk;
- Construction of a dry building mixes factory in the city of Yakutsk;
- Reconstruction of the Yakuttsement factory;
- Factory for the production of effective thermal insulation materials based on basalt resources located in the Billyakh deposit in Mokhsogollokh settlement;
- Production of the new Teplon construction, thermal insulation, and decorative material in Suntar Ulus;
- Development of the Mariika marble stone veneer deposit in the Neryungri area close to the existing railway and Amur-Yakutsk highway;
- Development of the Taloe granite deposit in Neryungri ulus;
- Development of the Nadezhda stone veneer deposit (South Yakutia);
- Development of the timber industry in the Sakha (Yakutia) Republic.

**Objects listed in the state programs:**
The Sakha (Yakutia) Republic State Program for "Gasification of human settlements and ensuring for gas supply reliability in the Sakha (Yakutia) Republic for the period from 2012 through 2016":

- Completion of the III branch of the main gas pipeline SVGKM-Mastakh-Berge-Yakutsk – Yakutsk (commissioning);

The Sakha (Yakutia) Republic State Program for "Development of the transportation system of the Sakha (Yakutia) Republic for the period from 2012 through 2016":

- Completion of the Berkakit-Tommot-Yakutsk railway line construction;
- Construction and reconstruction of Kolyma road segments (the road from Yakutsk to Magadan);
- Reconstruction of M-56 Lena road segments from Never to Yakutsk;

- Construction and reconstruction of Vilyui road segments – the road near the M-53 Baikal road through Bratsk, Ust-Kut, Mirny to Yakutsk;
- Amga road;
- Kobyai road;
- Aldan road.

State Program for "Regional economic policy of the Sakha (Yakutia) Republic for the period from 2012 through 2016":

- Development of the Tomponsky mining district (non-ferrous metallurgy, roads, overhead electric power transmission (OEPT) lines, and thermal power plants in Khandyga settlement);
- Development of deposits in South Yakutia (Sardana lead-zinc deposit, Kuranakh ore field, Lunnoe, Ryabinovoe, OEPT lines);
- Integrated development of South Yakutia (mining and processing iron ore, uranium and apatite, coal refining, OEPT lines, roads and railroads, Kankun hydropower plant);
- Integrated development of West Yakutia and Northern Irkutsk Oblast (oil and gas industry, diamond industry, Yakutia-Khabarovsk-Vladivostok highway, Vilyui road segments, OEPT lines);
- Creation of the mining cluster in Northern Yakutia (tin mining, extension of the Deputatskaya small thermal power station OEPT lines, electric power transmission lines, and Yana road);
- Creation of the coal cluster in South Yakutia (Elga, Denisovsk, Lokuchakitsk, Chulmakansk deposits);
- Creation of a special industrial economic zone.

## 2.3. KAMCHATKA KRAI

### 2.3.1. THE STRATEGY

On 27.07.2010 the Government of Kamchatka Krai approved the strategy of the socio-economic development of Kamchatka Krai through 2025 (No 332-P).

**Priorities:**

- Ensuring the competitiveness of the region by applying a cluster policy.

**Goals:**

- Creating conditions for the development of Kamchatka Krai's advanced economic specialization profile providing competitiveness on the basis of the region's economic geography, natural resources, industrial, human, and scientific potential within Federal and sectoral development strategies, and socio-economic development of the Russian Federation and municipalities' strategies and strategic programs for large companies;
- Forming a stable settlement system, which is based on territories of advanced economic growth with a high level of comfort for the population;
- Establishing a regulatory framework that defines price, tariff, customs, tax, and fiscal policies and provides economic growth; establishes the competitiveness of products, goods, and services in accordance with the selected economic specialization; and removes barriers to economic and social integration of the region with the international community, as well as active integration with the rest of Russia;
- Forming the population and labor force to the extent required to address economic challenges the region is facing and improving the quality of human capital;
- Preserving and supporting the traditional lifestyles of the Kamchatka region's indigenous minorities.

## 2.3.2. ACTION PLANS

The action plan to implement the Strategy is not presented.

## 2.3.3. STATE PROGRAMS

The list of Kamchatka Krai State Programs is shown in Table 2.2.

**TABLE 2.2.**   The List of Kamchatka Krai State Programs

| Number | Name of the state program |
|---|---|
| 1 | "Cultural development in Kamchatka Krai for the period from 2014 through 2018." |
| 2 | "Prevention of crime, terrorism, extremism, narcotism and alcoholism in Kamchatka Krai for the period from 2014 through 2018." |
| 3 | "Social security for citizens in Kamchatka Krai for the period from 2014 through 2018." |
| 4 | "Development of the information society in Kamchatka Krai for the period from 2014 through 2018." |
| 5 | "Development of agriculture, including agriculture regulations in Kamchatka Krai for the period from 2014 through 2018." |
| 6 | "Development of the economy and foreign economic activity of Kamchatka Krai for the period from 2014 through 2018." |
| 7 | "State finance management of Kamchatka Krai for the period from 2014 through 2018." |
| 8 | "Environmental protection and the usage of natural resources in Kamchatka Krai for the period from 2014 through 2018." |
| 9 | "Employment assistance program in Kamchatka Krai for the period from 2014 through 2018." |
| 10 | "Housing program in Kamchatka Krai for the period from 2014 through 2018." |
| 11 | "Implementation of the state national policies and growth of civil unity in Kamchatka Krai for the period from 2014 through 2018." |
| 12 | "Development of the transportation system in Kamchatka Krai for the period from 2014 through 2025." |
| 13 | "Protection of territories and population from emergencies; fire safety; development of civil defense and the support of Russian Cossacks in Kamchatka Krai for the period from 2014 through 2018." |
| 14 | "Development of tourism (including inner tourism) in Kamchatka Krai for the period from 2014 through 2018." |
| 15 | "Development of the education system in Kamchatka Krai for the period from 2014 through 2016." |
| 16 | "Development of the health system in Kamchatka Krai for the period from 2014 through 2020." |
| 17 | "Development of the electricity system, effective energy system and utilities services in Kamchatka Krai for the period from 2014 through 2018." |
| 18 | "Physical education, sports, youth politics, children's recreation and rehabilitation in Kamchatka Krai for the period from 2014 through 2018." |

**TABLE 3.2.** (Continued).

| Number | Name of the state program |
|--------|---------------------------|
| 19 | "Social and economic development of the "Korykskiy district" special status territory for the period from 2014 through 2020." |
| 20 | "Development of the fish industry in Kamchatka Krai for the period from 2014 through 2020." |
| 21 | "Improving the state property management in Kamchatka Krai for the period from 2014 through 2018." |

## 2.3.4. PROJECTS LISTED IN THE STRATEGY AND STATE PROGRAMS

### Projects listed in the Strategy of Kamchatka Krai:

- Avachinsk agglomeration;
- Petropavlovsk-Kamchatsky sea port;
- Paratunsky resort;
- Construction of the Trans-Kamchatka highway;
- Construction of Okha – Ust-Bolsheretsk, Ust-Bolsheretsk-Magadan high-speed fiber-optic lines (FOL);
- Construction of hydropower plants on Zhupanova river;
- Construction of a Geothermal Power Plant on the basis of the Mutnovsky deposit;
- Construction of the Yelizovo – Omsukchan railway line;
- Kamchatka Krai gas supply. The first priority is the Petropavlovsk-Kamchatsky gas supply;
- Development of Kamchatka-1 and Kamchatka-2 oil and gas fields;
- Construction of a floating nuclear power plant in the city of Vilyuchinsk;
- Creation of a bioresources cluster;
- Creation of the Avacha special economic port zone;
- Creation of a marine economic cluster;
- Creation of a special economic zone for tourism and recreation;
- Creation of a special economic zone that includes the whole territory of Kamchatka Krai;
- Creation of the development zone in Kamchatka Krai;

- Design and construction of the sea port terminal in the city of Petropavlovsk-Kamchatsky;
- Modernization of ZAO Petropavlovsk-Kamchatsky Shipyard;
- Modernization of ZAO Sudoremservis shipyard;
- Design and construction of a Petropavlovsk-Kamchatsky Shipyard hydraulic structure (dry dock) that measures 180 m long and 45 m wide;
- Project for waste-free titanium processing: magnetite sands of the Halatyrsk deposit at the mining and processing plant.

**Projects listed in the State Programs:**
Kamchatka Krai State Program for "Kamchatka Krai transportation system development during the period from 2014 through 2025":

- Construction and reconstruction of Milkovo – Klyuchi – Ust-Kamchatsk road;
- Construction and reconstruction of Petropavlovsk-Kamchatsky – Milkovo road;
- Construction of Anavgay settlement – Palana settlement prolonged operating winter road.

# 2.4. PRIMORSKY KRAI

## 2.4.1. THE STRATEGY

The strategy of Primorsky Krai's socio-economic development through 2025 was accepted by the Primorsky Krai legislature on 20.10.2008 (No 324-KZ).

**Priorities:**

- Improving Primorsky Krai economic competitiveness.

**Goals:**

- Developing the project on transportation and deep processing of hydrocarbon raw materials;

- Developing a transportation and logistics cluster;
- Developing processing sectors;
- Developing a fishery cluster;
- Developing a tourist cluster;
- Developing a shipbuilding and ship repair cluster;
- Developing innovative activity
- Developing the agricultural industry;
- Developing the mining and chemical industries;
- Developing the construction industry;
- Creating an urban agglomeration system around Vladivostok;
- Improving settlements' sustainability;
- Increasing human resources capitalization;
- Implementing infrastructure development programs.

## 2.4.2. ACTION PLANS

The action plan to implement the strategy of the socio-economic development of Primorsky Krai through 2025 includes the following:

- Improving the competitiveness of basic sectors of the economy and organization of effective clusters;
- Developing the project on transportation and deep processing of hydrocarbon raw materials;
- Developing a transportation and logistics cluster;
- Developing processing sectors;
- Developing a fishery cluster;
- Developing a tourist cluster;
- Developing a shipbuilding and ship repair cluster;
- Developing innovations;
- Developing other sectors of the economy;
- Enhancing the investment attraction mechanisms in Primorsky Krai;
- Institutionalizing a cluster policy;
- Improving settlements' sustainability;
- Implementing Vladivostok's agglomeration;
- Increasing human resources capitalization;

- Reforming the labor market;
- Implementing demographic policies and promoting migration incentives in Primorsky Krai;
- Developing pre-schools, as well as general and secondary education;
- Developing the health system;
- Developing the cultural sphere.
- Implementing infrastructure development programs:
- Developing the energy infrastructure;
- Developing the engineering infrastructure;
- Developing the environmental infrastructure.

## 2.4.3. STATE PROGRAMS

The list of Primorsky Krai State Programs is shown in Table 2.3.

**TABLE 2.3.**    The list of Primorsky Krai State Programs

| Number | Name of the state program |
|---|---|
| 1 | "Protection of territories and population from emergencies; fire safety; water objects safety in Primorsky Krai" for the period from 2013 through 2017. |
| 2 | "Information society" for the period from 2013 through 2017 |
| 3 | "Available housing and quality utilities for population program in Primorsky Krai" for the period from 2013 through 2017. |
| 4 | "Environment protection in Primorsky Krai" for the period from 2013 through 2017. |
| 5 | "Development of the health system in Primorsky Krai" for the period from 2013 through 2017. |
| 6 | "Cultural development in Primorsky Krai for the period from 2013 through 2017." |
| 7 | "Development of the forestry industry in Primorsky Krai" for the period from 2013 through 2017 |
| 8 | "Development of the education system in Primorsky Krai" for the period from 2013 through 2017 |
| 9 | "Development of the fishery complex in Primorsky Krai for the period from 2013 through 2017" |

**TABLE 2.3.** (Continued).

| Number | Name of the state program |
|--------|---------------------------|
| 10 | "Development of the agriculture industry? and regulation of the agriculture industry. Improving the life of the rural population in Primorsky Krai" for the period from 2013 through 2020. |
| 11 | "Development of the transportation system in Primorsky Krai" for the period from 2013 through 2017. |
| 12 | "Development of tourism in Primorsky Krai" for the period from 2013 through 2017. |
| 13 | "Development of physical education and sports in Primorsky Krai" for the period from 2013 through 2017. |
| 14 | "Employment assistance program in Primorsky Krai for the period from 2013 through 2017." |
| 15 | "Social support of the population in Primorsky Krai for the period from 2013 through 2017. |
| 16 | "Development of the economy and innovations in Primorsky Krai" for the period from 2013 through 2017. |
| 17 | "Energy effectiveness, gasification development and energy in Primorsky Krai" for the period from 2013 through 2017. |

## 2.4.4. PROJECTS LISTED IN THE STRATEGY AND STATE PROGRAMS

### Projects listed in the Primorsky Krai Strategy:

- Construction of the Eastern Siberia–Pacific Ocean oil pipeline;
- Construction of Vostochny oil refinery;
- Creation of the gas transportation system;
- Construction of a gas refinery;
- Construction of a liquefied and natural gas production plant;
- Construction of a mineral fertilizers production factory;
- Establishing the industrial port zone and layered port on the basis of the existing ports of Vostochny and Nakhodka;
- Development of a Vostochny – Nakhodka port system;
- Development of the port in Kozmino Bay (regional port specializing in oil and oil products export);

- Development of the port in the Bay of Suhodol (specializing in coal transit);
- Development of the port in the Trinity Bay (regional port specializing in coal, container and other goods transit, including transit from China);
- Development of the Vladivostok transport node (specializing in container and horizontal cargo handling);
- Development of Vladivostok International Airport (creating a large transportation hub);
- Reconstruction of the M60 Ussuri federal highway from Khabarovsk to Vladivostok;
- Completion of the federal highway from Khabarovsk to Nakhodka;
- Development of Transsiberian, Primorye-1, Primorye-2 international transport corridors;
- Construction of the gas pipeline from Khabarovsk to Vladivostok;
- Organization of the Dalnevostochny Logistichesky Tsentr transport and distribution center in Hmylovka settlement;
- Construction of the Yuzniy Primorskiy Terminal transport and logistics complex in Nadezhda district;
- Creation of logistic centers for Russian Railways in areas of interface with differently gauged lines and in Pacific Coast seaports, as well as the construction of a logistics center in North East China;
- Organization of large logistic nodes in the cities of Ussuriisk and Artyom;
- Integrated development of the Grodekovo-Suifenhe railway border crossing;
- Integrated development of the Makhalino (Kamyshovaya) – Hunchun railway border crossing;
- Construction of the Turiy Rog – Mishan railway border crossing;
- Construction of the Lesozavodsk – Hulin railway crossing including expanding of the Lesozavodsk – Dalnegorsk – Rudnaya Pristan railway line;
- Organization of a modern fish market in Vladivostok;
- Creation of the Pacific Center for Biotechnology;
- Creation of a sea biotech park;

- Creation of the Far Eastern center of the United Shipbuilding Corporation;
- Development of the Far Eastern Federal University;
- Creation of the Far Eastern State Marine Science Complex (on the basis of the Maritime State University);
- Construction of the Ussuriisk power plant;
- Construction of mobile gas turbine power plants on the Vladivostok TPP-1 territory;
- Construction of Vladivostok TPP-3;
- Reconstruction of Vladivostok TPP-2 with a transition to gas fuel combustion;
- Reconstruction of the Artyem TPP (including installation of new power units);
- Construction of a new power plant in the Nadezhda district;
- Expansion and reconstruction of the Partisansk power station;
- Construction of a nuclear power plant.

**Projects listed in the State Programs:**
Primorsky Krai State Program for "Primorsky Krai fishery system development during the period from 2013 through 2017":

- Development and implementation of the pilot project on the fish processing cluster;
- Development and implementation of the pilot project on the auction-based trading platform;
- Creation of the fish market in the city of Vladivostok and in the other cities of Primorsky Krai.

Primorsky Krai State Program for "Primorsky Krai transportation system development during the 2013–2017 period":

- Construction of the Vladivostok – Nakhodka – Vostochny port road;
- Construction of the road from the Khabarovsk – Vladivostok federal road to the Vladivostok – Nakhodka – Vostochny port road.

Primorsky Krai State Program of "Primorsky Krai tourist system development during the period from 2013 through 2017":

- Development of the Vladivostok Center for Business Tourism recreation and tourism cluster;
- Creation of the Pidan tourism and recreation cluster;
- Creation of the Ussuriisk – Mikhailovka tourism and recreation cluster;
- Creation of the Arseniev tourism and recreation cluster;
- Development of the Shmakovsky tourism and recreation cluster project;
- Creation of the Nakhodka – Partizansk tourism and recreation cluster;
- Creation of the Khasansky border cluster.

## 2.5. KHABAROVSK KRAI

### 2.5.1. THE STRATEGY

Strategy for the social and economic development of Khabarovsk Krai through 2025 approved by the Instruction of the Government of Khabarovsk Krai N 1 – pr. Dated 13.01.2009.

**Priorities:**

- Improving the region's competitiveness

**Goals:**

- Forming a comfortable and safe living environment in the region;
- Forming a competitive economic complex;
- Integrating into the Asia Pacific economic system as a whole and into the North East Asia economic system in particular;
- Creating economic and social frameworks for adequate modern socio-economic development goals.

### 2.5.2. ACTION PLANS

The action plan to implement the Strategy is not presented.

## 2.5.3. STATE PROGRAMS

The list of Khabarovsk Krai state programs is shown in Table 2.4.

**TABLE 2.4.**     The List of Khabarovsk Krai State Programs

| Number | Name of the state program |
|---|---|
| 1 | "Development of social security in Khabarovsk Krai" |
| 2 | "Environment protection and ecological security in Khabarovsk Krai" |
| 3 | "Development of tourism in Khabarovsk Krai for the period from 2013 through 2020" |
| 4 | "Development of the housing industry in Khabarovsk Krai" |
| 5 | "Maintain public safety and crime prevention in Khabarovsk Krai" |
| 6 | "Culture of Khabarovsk Krai" |
| 7 | "Business and investment climate improvement in Khabarovsk Krai" |
| 8 | "Development of the information society in Khabarovsk Krai" |
| 9 | "Emergency and fire protection of the population in Khabarovsk Krai" |
| 10 | "Development of the health system in Khabarovsk Krai" |
| 11 | "Development of the water-economic system in Khabarovsk Krai for the period from 2014 through 2020" |
| 12 | "Energy effectiveness and development of energy in Khabarovsk Krai" |
| 13 | "State finance management of Khabarovsk Krai" |
| 14 | "Development of the indigenous people of the North, Siberia and the Far East of the Russian Federation, that live in Khabarovsk Krai" |
| 15 | "Development of the small and medium business in Khabarovsk Krai for the period from 2013 through 2020" |
| 16 | "Innovation and modernization of the economy of Khabarovsk Krai" |
| 17 | "Development of the education system in Khabarovsk Krai" |
| 18 | "Assisting voluntary resettlement to Khabarovsk Krai of compatriots living abroad" |
| 19 | "Development of agriculture and the regulation of the agriculture industry in Khabarovsk Krai for the period from 2013 through 2020" |
| 20 | "Affordable environment" |
| 21 | "Development of the transportation system in Khabarovsk Krai" |
| 22 | "Assisting the development of the local government system in Khabarovsk Krai" |
| 23 | "Development of the forest industry in Khabarovsk Krai" |
| 24 | "Development of physical education, sports and youth political activity in Khabarovsk Krai" |

**TABLE 2.4.** (Continued).

| Number | Name of the state program |
|--------|---------------------------|
| 25 | "Developing the job market and providing job search assistance to the population of Khabarovsk Krai" |
| 26 | "Development of the hunting industry, protection of the animal world and maintenance of national parks in Khabarovsk Krai" |
| 27 | "Development of the fish industry in Khabarovsk Krai" |
| 28 | "Public property management in Khabarovsk Krai" |
| 29 | "Improving the living standards of the population in Khabarovsk Krai" |
| 30 | "Assisting the development of civil society in Khabarovsk Krai for the period from 2013 through 2020" |
| 31 | "Strategic planning and the improvement of labor capacity in Khabarovsk Krai" |

## *2.5.4. PROJECTS LISTED IN THE STRATEGY AND STATE PROGRAMS*

Projects listed in the Strategy of Khabarovsk Krai:

- Developing new ore deposits in Avlayakan (Ayano-Maisky District), Kirankan (Tuguro-Chumikansky District), Svetle (Okhotsky District), Kutyn (Tuguro-Chumikansky District), Belaya Gora (Nikolaevsky District), Delken (Ulchsky District), Durmin (Lazo District), Noni (Verkhnebureinsky District) and in other Districts;
- Developing a mining complex at the Albazino deposit of the Polina Osipenko District;
- Amursk city hydrometallurgy plant, which processes gold ore concentrate coming from the mining complex at the Albazino deposit;
- Pravourmiyskoye tin ore deposit;
- Increasing the capacity of the processing factory located at the Pravourmiyskoye deposit, as well as developing the Krasivaya zone of the Festival deposit and Silinskaya zone of the Perevalnoe deposit;
- Opening the Soboliny tin ore deposit in 2015;
- Developing the Amurmetall JSC steel plant complex;
- Constructing an aluminum factory producing primary aluminum;
- Creating the Pacific Coast center for the deep processing of wood;
- Komsomolsk-on-Amur Aircraft Production Association JSC;

- Amur shipbuilding Plant JSC;
- Khabarovsk shipbuilding Plant JSC (construction of hovercraft ships and high-speed ships);
- Amur Cable Plant JSC;
- Komsomolsk-on-Amur Handling equipment Plant JSC;
- Dalenergomash JSC;
- Komsomolsk oil refinery (LLC RN – Komsomolsky NPZ);
- Khabarovsk NPZ JSC;
- Constructing the central TPP in the city of Sovetskaya Gavan;
- Constructing the Urgalsk TPP;
- East Siberia – Pacific Ocean oil pipeline system;
- Creating the Far Eastern oil pipeline system included in the Sakhalin – Komsomolsk-on-Amur, East Siberia – Pacific Ocean – Komsomolsk oil refinery and East Siberia – Pacific Ocean – Khabarovsk oil refinery systems;
- Constructing the Sakhalin – Khabarovsk – Vladivostok gas pipeline system;
- Constructing the Yakutia – Khabarovsk – Vladivostok gas pipeline;
- Sovetskaya Gavan seaport special economic zone;
- De-Kastri – Vanino – Sovetskaya Gavan port transit zone;
- Creating an international air hub in the Khabarovsk international Airport (Novyi);
- Creating a Khabarovsk – Fuyuan cargo and passenger checkpoint at the state border located on Bolshoy Ussurisky Island;
- Constructing the Kuznetsov railroad tunnel;
- Developing the De-Kastri port (constructing the oil and gas cargo terminal; constructing a pipeline from Komsomolsk oil and gas refinery to the port);
- Komsomolsk-on-Amur Aircraft Production Association JSC, branch of SCA, Sukhoi Civil Aircraft.

**Projects listed in state programs:**
"Development of the tourism industry in Khabarovsk Krai for the period from 2013 through 2020" Khabarovsk Krai state program:

- Creation of the tourism and recreation complex in Amursk municipal district;

- Creation of the cultural and tourism complex in the Dzhuyen settlement of the Amursk municipal district;
- Development of the infrastructure of the Russkaya Derevnya tourism and cultural complex in the Khabarovsk municipal district;
- Maintenance of the tourism and recreation zone in the Petropavlovka settlement of the Khabarovsk municipal district;
- Creation of the Ozero Lotosov tourism and recreation zone in the Khabarovsk municipal district;
- Creation of the Bolshoy Ussuriysky Island – Shantary cruise cluster;
- Creation of the Severny Sikhote – Alin tourism and recreation cluster;
- "Development of the transportation system in Khabarovsk Krai" state program;
- Construction of the Khabarovsk – Lidoga – Vanino road with an exit to the city of Komsomolk-on-Amur;
- Construction of the Selikhino – Nikolayevsk-on-Amur road;
- Construction of the Ayan – Nelkan – Yugorenok (the border of the Sakha (Yakutia) Republic) road.

"Development of the Fish industry in Khabarovsk Krai" state program:

- Development of aquaculture and the reproduction of marine biological resources in the region;
- Organization of fish facilities and commercial fish farming in the region;
- Development of coastal processing of aquatic biological resources in the region;
- Construction and modernization of private fish processing facilities and fish products storage facilities in the region.

## 2.6. AMUR OBLAST

### 2.6.1. THE STRATEGY

Strategy for the social and economic development of Amur Oblast through 2025 approved by the Instruction of the Government of Amur Oblast N 380. Dated 13.07.2012.

**Priorities:**

- Competitive specialization of the region's economy in the interregional and international division of labor.

**Goals:**

- Forming a diversified economic structure with a high level of added value on the basis of modern innovations;
- Developing a major agricultural base to implement food security of the Pacific Coast region;
- Advanced development of infrastructure for accelerated socio-economic development;
- Environmental protection;
- Achieving the national average level of housing and social infrastructure availability for the population.

## 2.6.2. ACTION PLANS

The strategy implementation plan includes a set of measures aimed at creating conditions for effective economic development in regions, including:

- Creating a private equity fund, industrial parks, and special economic zones;
- Implementing a price and tariff policy that provides competitiveness of products (works, services);
- Developing a set of measures for the basic forms of economical specialization;
- Constructing the Vostochny Cosmodrome;
- Gasification;
- Developing a set of measures to create conditions that attract human resources and create favorable conditions for human residence;
- Developing a set of measures to develop the BAM zone;
- Improving border checkpoints.

## 2.6.3. STATE PROGRAMS

The list of Amur Oblast state programs is shown in Table 2.5.

**TABLE 2.5.**   The List of Amur Oblast State Programs

| Number | Name of the state program |
|--------|---------------------------|
| 1 | "Development of agriculture and the regulation of the agriculture industry in Amur Oblast for the period from 2013 through 2020" |
| 2 | "Development of social security in Amur Oblast for the period from 2014 through 2020" |
| 3 | "Development and protection of the culture and art of Amur Oblast for the period from 2014 through 2020" |
| 4 | "Environmental protection in Amur Oblast for the period from 2014 through 2020" |
| 5 | "Modernization of housing and communal services, energy conservation and energy efficiency in Amur Oblast for the period from 2014 through 2020" |
| 6 | "Development of the health system in Amur Oblast for the period from 2014 through 2020" |
| 7 | "Development of affordable housing in Amur Oblast for the period from 2014 through 2020" |
| 8 | "Development of the economy and innovative economy in Amur Oblast for the period from 2014 through 2020" |
| 9 | "Development of physical education and sports in Amur Oblast for the period from 2014 through 2020" |
| 10 | "Improving the efficiency of public authorities and management of the Amur Region for the period from 2014 through 2020" |
| 11 | "Risk reduction and mitigation of natural and man-made disasters, as well as the public safety field for the period from 2014 through 2020" |
| 12 | "Development of the education system in Amur Oblast for the period from 2014 through 2020" |
| 13 | "Development of the transportation system in Amur Oblast for the period from 2014 through 2020" |

## 2.6.4. PROJECTS, LISTED IN STRATEGIES AND STATE PROGRAMS

Projects, listed in the strategy of Amur Oblast:

- Constructing the second stage of Blagoveshchensk central TPP;
- Constructing the Erkovetsk TPP;
- Creating gas processing and gas chemical complexes;

- Developing the Ogodzhinsky stone coal deposit;
- Constructing the Vostochny Cosmodrome;
- Reconstructing the entrance to the Amur (Chita -Khabarovsk) federal highway to Blagoveshchensk and constructing a road bridge over the Zeya river;
- Constructing a bridge across Selemdzha river on the 303rd km of Vvedenovka – Fevralsk – Ekimchan road;
- Constructing a road bridge over Amur river between Blagoveshchensk (Russia) to Heihe (PRC);
- Terminal-based logistical center in Blagoveshchensk;
- Terminal-based logistical center in Poyarkovo settlement;
- Constructing the Shimanovsk – Chagoyan – Gar – Fevralsk – Ogodzha railway with a length of 439 km;
- Constructing the railway bridge across Amur river between Dzhalinda (RF) and Mohe (PRC);
- Constructing the railway bridge across the Amur river between Blagoveshchensk (Russia) and Heihe (PRC);
- Constructing and reconstructing the Ignatievo airport complex in Blagoveshchensk;
- Developing the Malyi Kurumkan, Vodorazdelnaya, Sobolevskaya copper-nickel ore deposits and the Kun-Maniyo ore mining and processing enterprise;
- Developing the Evgenevskoye apatite deposit;
- Bureysky hatchery in Bureysky District;
- Zeisky hatchery in Zeya district;
- Organizing pork production in pig farming with the capacity of 58,200 heads per year in the Srednebeloe settlement of the Ivanovo district (LLC Amurinvestprodukt);
- Developing the engineering infrastructure of industrial production in the Belogorsk special economic zone;
- Chigirinsky agriculture park;
- Amur technical innovation center in the city of Blagoveshchensk.

**Objects listed in state programs:**
- "Economic development and innovation of Amur Oblast for the period from 2014 through 2020" state program:

- A biopharmaceutical factory that produces innovative products based on Taxifolin.

## 2.7. MAGADAN OBLAST

## *2.7.1. THE STRATEGY*

The strategy for the social and economic development of Magadan Oblast through 2025.

**Priorities:**

- Forming a competitive economic model, based on existing regional strengths and resources and the favorable living conditions of the population.

**Goals:**

- Forming a stable system of resettlement, based on regional zones of advancing economic growth;
- Creating conditions for the development of promising economic specialization based on natural resources, manufacturing, human resources, the scientific potential of the region in the framework of interrelated federal branched development strategies, the socio-economic development of municipal formations, and the strategic programs of large companies;
- Assisting the implementation of the most significant investment projects to the region;
- Increasing the flow of investment into the region;
- Creating favorable conditions for the development of small and medium businesses and assisting the improvement of the business climate for private sector development;
- Establishing a regulatory framework that defines special conditions for price, tariff, customs, tax, and fiscal policies aimed at ensuring economic growth and improving the competitiveness of products, goods, and services according to the economic specialization;

- Developing human potential (improving the competitiveness of human resources, in the labor and social sectors, as well as improving the quality of the social environment and living conditions).

## 2.7.2. ACTION PLANS

"The strategy of social and economic development of Magadan Oblast for the period up to 2025" provides the following actions:

- Diversifying the economy to ensure its competitiveness in the following areas:
  - Mining;
  - Developing the energy sector;
  - Developing the construction industry;
  - Developing transport infrastructure;
  - Developing the fishing industry;
  - Developing agriculture;
  - Expanding the scope of the special economic zone;
  - Introducing innovations;
  - Attracting investments;
  - Developing small business.
- Developing the social sphere:
  - Developing the education system;
  - Developing the health care system;
  - Developing culture;
  - Developing sports and tourism;
  - Employment;
  - Youth policy;
  - Developing trade.
- Environmental security in the region:
  - Rational use of forest resources;
  - Protecting wildlife;
  - Fire safety.
- Improving management and implementing digital technologies.
- Financial support.

## 2.7.3. STATE PROGRAMS

The list of Magadan Oblast state programs is shown in Table 2.6.

**TABLE 2.6.**   The List of Magadan Oblast State Programs

| Number | Name of the state program |
|--------|---------------------------|
| 1 | "Development of the health care system in Magadan Oblast" |
| 2 | "Development of the education system in Magadan Oblast" |
| 3 | "Youth of Magadan Oblast" |
| 4 | "Development of culture in Magadan Oblast" |
| 5 | "Development of physical education, sports and tourism in Magadan Oblast" |
| 6 | "Public safety, crime and corruption prevention, combating narcotics trafficking in Magadan Oblast" |
| 7 | "Protection of territories and population from emergencies, and fire safety in Magadan Oblast" |
| 8 | "Natural resources and ecology in Magadan Oblast" |
| 9 | "Forming an affordable environment in Magadan Oblast" |
| 10 | "Labor forces in Magadan Oblast" |
| 11 | "Labor protection in Magadan Oblast" |
| 12 | "Social security of the population in Magadan Oblast" |
| 13 | "An affordable and comfortable housing program in Magadan Oblast" |
| 14 | "Development of the state and municipal management system in Magadan Oblast" |
| 15 | "Aiding the development of civil society, interethnic harmony and patriotism in Magadan Oblast" |
| 16 | "Development of aquaculture in Magadan Oblast" |
| 17 | "Conservation and reproduction of wildlife, including specially protected natural territories of regional importance in Magadan Oblast" |
| 18 | "Development of economy and innovation in Magadan Oblast" |
| 19 | "Development of an information society in Magadan Oblast" |
| 20 | "Development of the transportation system in Magadan Oblast" |
| 21 | "Development of the forest industry in Magadan Oblast" |
| 22 | "The development of building materials, products and designs industrial enterprises in Magadan Oblast" |

**TABLE 2.6.** (Continued).

| Number | Name of the state program |
|--------|---------------------------|
| 23 | "Energy conservation and energy efficiency in Magadan Oblast" |
| 24 | "Development of agriculture in Magadan Oblast" |
| 25 | "Development of foreign trade activities of Magadan Oblast and support of compatriots living abroad" |
| 26 | "Assisting municipalities in Magadan Oblast in the implementation of municipal programs for the integrated development of communal infrastructure" |
| 27 | "Ensuring the quality of housing and utilities services, and comfortable living conditions in Magadan Oblast" |
| 28 | "The resettlement of citizens from the residential premises in apartment buildings that were recognized as being in a state of emergency in the prescribed manner before January 1, 2012, and that are subject to demolition or reconstruction due to natural wear in the course of their operation, with the involvement of public corporations – Assistance in housing reformation fund" |
| 29 | "Socio-economic and cultural development of the indigenous people living on the territory of Magadan Oblast" |

## 2.7.4. PROJECTS, LISTED IN STRATEGIES AND STATE PROGRAMS

### Projects, listed in the Strategy of Magadan Oblast:

- Reconstructing Magadan Airport;
- Reconstructing the Magadan sea trading port;
- Constructing the Yakutsk – Magadan railway line;
- Reconstructing the Palatka – Kulu – Neksikan road;
- Reconstructing the Kolyma federal highway;
- Reconstructing the central TPP in Magadan;
- Constructing the Ust-Srednekanskaya hydropower plant.

### Projects, listed in state programs:

"Development of aquaculture in Magadan Oblast" state program:

- Construction, reconstruction and modernization of salmon hatcheries.

"Energy conservation and energy efficiency in the Magadan Oblast" state program:

- Construction of the Ust-Srednekanskaya hydro power plant.

# 2.8. SAKHALIN OBLAST

## 2.8.1. THE STRATEGY

Strategy for the socio-economic development of Sakhalin Oblast through 2025 approved by the Instruction of the Government of Sakhalin Oblast N99. Dated 28.03.2011.

**Priority:**

- Diversifying the economy and insuring its competitiveness.

**Goals:**

- Creating conditions for the development of promising economic specialization of Sakhalin Oblast.

According to the methodology used in this book, the purposes of the strategy are not defined.

## 2.8.2. ACTION PLANS

The action plan to implement the strategy is not presented.

## 2.8.3. STATE PROGRAMS

The list of state programs in Sakhalin Oblast for the period from 2014 through 2020 approved by the Instruction of the Government of Sakhalin Oblast N 99, "Socio-economic development strategy of Sakhalin Oblast for the period until 2025" on 28.03.2011, is shown in Table 2.7.

According to the Instruction of the Government of the Sakhalin Oblast N10 from 01.15.2014: "On amending the Instruction of the Government of the Sakhalin Oblast N99 from 28.03.2011 – 'Socio-economic development strategy of Sakhalin Oblast for the period until 2025' – all long-term target programs of the Sakhalin Oblast shall cease to apply on January 1, 2014.

**TABLE 2.7.**   The List of Sakhalin Oblast State Programs for the Period From 2014 Through 2020

| Number | Name of the state program |
|--------|----------------------------|
| 1 | "Development of the education system in Sakhalin Oblast for the period from 2014 through 2020" |
| 2 | "Improving public property management in Sakhalin Oblast for the period from 2014 through 2020" |
| 3 | "Information society in Sakhalin Oblast for the period from 2014 through 2020" |
| 4 | "Improving the government management system in Sakhalin Oblast for the period from 2014 through 2020" |
| 5 | "Economic development and innovations in Sakhalin Oblast for the period from 2014 through 2020" |
| 6 | "Industrial development in Sakhalin Oblast for the period from 2014 through 2020" |
| 7 | "Development of agriculture and the regulation of the agricultural industry in Sakhalin Oblast for the period from 2014 through 2020" |
| 8 | "Development of the transportation industry in Sakhalin Oblast for the period from 2014 through 2020" |
| 9 | "Public safety, crime prevention and combating narcotics trafficking in Sakhalin Oblast for the period from 2013 through 2020" |
| 10 | "Ensuring the quality of housing and utilities services in Sakhalin Oblast for the period from 2014 through 2020" |
| 11 | "Affordable environment in Sakhalin Oblast for the period from 2014 through 2020" |
| 12 | "Quality housing program in Sakhalin Oblast for the period from 2014 through 2020" |
| 13 | "Social security of the population in Sakhalin Oblast for the period from 2014 through 2020" |
| 14 | "Development of physical education, sports, tourism and improvement in youth policy in Sakhalin Oblast for the period from 2014 through 2020" |
| 15 | "Cultural development in Sakhalin Oblast for the period from 2014 through 2020" |

**TABLE 2.7.** (Continued).

| Number | Name of the state program |
|--------|---------------------------|
| 16 | "Development of the health care system in Sakhalin Oblast for the period from 2014 through 2020" |
| 17 | "Environment protection, conservation and reproduction of natural resources in Sakhalin Oblast for the period from 2014 through 2020" |
| 18 | "Development of the job market in Sakhalin Oblast for the period from 2014 through 2020" |
| 19 | "State finance management in Sakhalin Oblast for the period from 2014 through 2020" |
| 20 | "Development of international and inner-regional activities in Sakhalin Oblast for the period from 2014 through 2020" |
| 21 | "Development of the forest industry in Sakhalin Oblast for the period from 2014 through 2020" |
| 22 | "Development of the fishing industry in Sakhalin Oblast for the period from 2014 through 2020" |
| 23 | "Protection from natural and man-made disasters, fire protection, as well as public safety on water objects for the period from 2014 through 2020" |

## 2.8.4. PROJECTS LISTED IN THE STRATEGY AND STATE PROGRAMS

**Projects, listed in the strategy of the social and economic development of the Far East and Baikal regions for the period until 2025:**

- The ferry from Vanino to Kholmsk;
- Sakhalin railroad;
- Yuzhno-Sakhalinsk Airport;
- Special economic zone of the port type in Kholmsk and Nevelsk;
- Sakhalin – Khabarovsk – Vladivostok gas transportation system (provided with gas from Sakhalin-1 and Sakhalin-2);
- Sakhalin HPP-2;
- Sakhalin-3 project;
- Yuzhno-Sakhalinsk central TPP-1;
- Ilinsky and Korsakov seaports;
- New seaport in the area of the Nabil settlement.

**Projects listed in the Strategy of socio-economic development of Sakhalin Oblast until 2025:**

- Selikhino (Khabarovsk Krai) – Nysh (Sakhalin Oblast) railway line with a tunnel (bridge) through the Nevelsk Strait;
- Korsakov, Kholmsk, Uglegorsk, Shahtersk, Boshnyakovo, Aleksandrovsk-Sakhalinsk seaports;
- Yuzhno-Kurilsk, Kuril, Severo-Kurilsk port stations;
- A ferry system from Vanino to Kholmsk in the Kholmsk seaport (including the construction of two vehicle and train ferries);
- Ilyinsky and Nevelsk seaports;
- New seaport in the area of Nabil settlement;
- Yuzhno-Sakhalinsk, Zonal, Okha and Mendeleevo (Kunashir Island), Iturup (Iturup Island) airports;
- South Sakhalin central TPP-1;
- Sakhalin HPP-2.

**Projects listed in federal programs:**
"Socio-economic development of Kuril Islands (Sakhalin Oblast) for the period from 2007 through 2015" federal target program:

- Kuril port station in the Kitovyi Bay on Iturup Island.
- Salmon hatcheries for the production of juvenile pink and chum salmon on Iturup, Kunashir, and Paramushir islands.

"Economic and social development of the Far East and the Baikal region for the period until 2018" federal target program:

- A ferry system from Vanino to Kholmsk in the Kholmsk seaport (including the construction of two vehicle and train ferries).

**Projects listed in the state programs of Sakhalin Oblast:**
"Economic development and innovation policy of Sakhalin Oblast for the period from 2014 -through 2020" state program:

- Reconstruction of cargo-passenger complex in Kuril port in Kitovyi Bay on Iturup Island;
- Construction of the Zelenoye Ozero tourist complex with mineral springs on Iturup Island;

- Construction of salmon hatcheries for the production of juvenile pink and chum salmon on Etorofu and Paramushir islands;
- Creation of Marine Biotech Park in the Sakhalin-Kuril territorial basin (construction of maritime industry and maintenance of onshore base in Golovnino settlement on Kunashir Island);
- Creation of a fishing industry cluster on Shikotan Island;
- Creation of an agro-industrial park on the Kuril Islands, including: the construction of greenhouses for the cultivation of fruits and vegetables.

"Industrial development in Sakhalin Oblast for the period until 2020" state program:

- Sakhalin – 1, Sakhalin – 2, Sakhalin – 3 projects;
- Development of deposits by Rosneft;
- Development of Okruzhnoe deposit;
- Construction of a new LNG plant on Sakhalin Island;
- Development of projects that create and implement high-tech processing industries (oil refining and gas chemistry).

"Development of the electricity industry of Sakhalin Oblast" sub-program N 1:

- Nogliki gas power station;
- South Sakhalin central TPP-1;
- Okhinskaya TPP;
- Sakhalin HPP-2.

"Gasification of the Sakhalin area" sub-program N 2:

- Construction of four equipped gas wells on the Aniva gas field.

"Development of the transport infrastructure and road facilities of Sakhalin Oblast for the period from 2014 through 2020" state program.

- Okha, Zonalnoe and Shahtersk airfield;
- Yuzhno-Sakhalinsk Airport;
- Investment projects of Sakhalin Oblast;

- Construction of the railway line from Ilinsk to Uglegorsk;
- Construction of the railway line from Selihin to Nysh with a crossing through Nevelsky Strait;
- Creation of oil and gas chemical production in Sakhalin Oblast;
- Construction of a passenger terminal in Yuzhno-Sakhalinsk Airport;
- Construction of the 4th unit at Yuzhno-Sakhalinsk central TPP-1.

## 2.9. JEWISH AUTONOMOUS OBLAST

### 2.9.1. THE STRATEGY

Strategy for the socio-economic development of Jewish Autonomous Oblast for the period through 2020 (Instructions of the Government of Jewish Autonomous Oblast N118-PP. Dated 20.03.2012).

**Priorities:**

- Improving the competitiveness of the region in terms of global market integration.

**Goals:**

- Creating the infrastructure for deposits ready to be developed;
- Implementing projects focused on the construction of a mining complex in the region to organize a supply chain for the Russian domestic market and for export;
- Increasing the integration of the region into the global transportation system;
- Ensuring accessibility to the transportation network for effective development deposits;
- Reducing disparities in transportation availability for different population areas;
- Increasing industry's revenue through the development of logistics;
- Improving the quality of road infrastructure;
- Promoting the deep processing of wood;

- Developing the furniture-production industry;
- Maintaining rational waste disposal of the forest industry by organizing the production of fuel pellets and creating a small-scale energy system that uses pellets as the main energy supply;
- Developing the wood panel production industry by using modern technologies;
- Implementing measures to restore forest resources;
- Organizing the production of construction materials that will be used during the construction of washing/enrichment plants and mining and metallurgical integrated plants;
- Changing the structure of agriculture in order to increase its effectiveness. In particular, stimulate the development of livestock and soy crop production;
- Achieving a deeper level of agricultural production processing in the region;
- Developing separate entities and components in inner-regional production cooperation on the basis of mining and steel plants;
- Creating new objects of tourist infrastructure to meet modern quality standards;
- Expanding the range of services offered;
- Promoting tourist services in the region on the Chinese market;
- Providing the infrastructure for the local population during weekend breaks.

## 2.9.2. ACTION PLANS

The action plan to implement the strategy is not presented.

## 2.9.3. STATE PROGRAMS

The list of Jewish Autonomous Oblast's state programs that are subject to state financing in 2014 and the planned period from 2015 until 2016 is shown in Table 2.8.

**TABLE 2.8.**   A List of State Programs of Jewish Autonomous Oblast to be Financed From the Regional Budget in 2014, As Well As in the Planned Period From 2015 Through 2016

| Number | Name of the state program |
|---|---|
| 1 | "Development of the road system in Jewish Autonomous Oblast for the period from 2014 through 2016" |
| 2 | "Development of agriculture and the regulation of the agricultural industry in Jewish Autonomous Oblast for the period from 2014 through 2020" |
| 3 | "Ensuring the quality of housing and utility services in Jewish Autonomous Oblast for the period from 2014 through 2016" |
| 4 | "Energy conservation and development of energy efficiency in Jewish Autonomous Oblast for the period from 2010 through 2020" |
| 5 | "The resettlement of citizens from the residential premises in apartment buildings that were recognized as being in a state of emergency, including the development of low-rise housing in Jewish Autonomous Oblast for the period from 2013 through 2017" |
| 6 | "Civil defense in Jewish Autonomous Oblast for the period from 2014 through 2017" |
| 7 | "Development of the education system in Jewish Autonomous Oblast for the period from 2014 through 2018" |
| 8 | "Social assistance in Jewish Autonomous Oblast for the period from 2014 through 2016" |
| 9 | "Affordable environment in Jewish Autonomous Oblast for the period from 2014 through 2016" |
| 10 | "Development of the health care system in Jewish Autonomous Oblast for the period from 2014 through 2018" |
| 11 | "Development of culture and sports in Jewish Autonomous Oblast for the period from 2014 through 2016" |
| 12 | "Assisting voluntary resettlement to Jewish Autonomous Oblast of compatriots living abroad for the period from 2013 through 2017" |
| 13 | "Public and road safety in Jewish Autonomous Oblast for the period from 2014 through 2018" |
| 14 | "Forming a good investment climate in Jewish Autonomous Oblast for the period from 2014 through 2018" |
| 15 | "Ecology of Jewish Autonomous Oblast for the period from 2014 through 2025" |
| 16 | "Development of the water economic system in Jewish Autonomous Oblast" |
| 17 | "Labor availability and labor safety for the period from 2014 through 2016" |

**TABLE 2.8.** (Continued).

| Number | Name of the state program |
|--------|---------------------------|
| 18 | "Introduction of satellite navigation technology with the GLONASS system and other results of space activities for the socio-economic and innovative development of Jewish Autonomous Oblast for the period from 2013 through 2016" |
| 19 | "Formation of an information society and development of the digital government in Jewish Autonomous Oblast for the period from 2014 through 2016" |
| 20 | "Cadastral land evaluation in Jewish Autonomous Oblast for the period from 2016 through 2018" |

## 2.9.4. PROJECTS, LISTED IN THE STRATEGY AND STATE PROGRAMS

### Projects listed in the strategy of Jewish Autonomous Oblast:

- Constructing the Kimkano-Sutarsky mining processing plant;
- Constructing Dalnevostochny metallurgichesky zavod (Far Eastern steel factory);
- Reconstructing Teploozersky tsementny zavod JSC (Teploozersk cement factory);
- Creating a special economic zone near the Nizhneleninskoye border checkpoint (10 square km. in area);
- Transferring the operating system using boilers to the new NTV combustion technology system in Birobidzhan central TPP;
- Constructing a pig farm for 54,000 heads in Smidovich settlement;
- Organizing an enterprise for the deep processing of wood in Pashkovo settlement;
- Organizing an enterprise for the deep processing of wood in Nizhne-Leninsky settlement;
- Creating and modernizing the forest industry infrastructure.

### Projects listed in the state programs:

"Introduction of satellite navigation technology with the GLONASS system and other results of space activities for the socio-economic and innovative development of the Jewish Autonomous Oblast for the period from 2013 through 2016" state program:

- Creation of the regional road navigation system using the GLONASS system to provide services in Jewish Autonomous Oblast and to provide the GLONASS system to certain transportation vehicles;
- Creation of a regional geographic information system within Jewish Autonomous Oblast that provides an integrated infrastructure using data from spatial maps and Jewish Autonomous Oblast infrastructure.

## 2.10. CHUKOTKA AUTONOMOUS OKRUG

### 2.10.1. THE STRATEGY

Developing mining industries and conducting geological surveys for effective mining have been outlined as strategic directions for the economic activity in Chukotka Autonomous Okrug while taking into account the special features of territories in the Far North. The development of industrial production and infrastructure will be concentrated in two areas of advancing economic growth located in Anadyr and Chaun-Bilibinsk.[3]

The basic direction of economic activity in the region is defined by the development of mining industries, focusing on a more complete and efficient development of mineral resources concentrated in two industrial areas of advanced development: Anadyr and Chaun-Bilibinsk.[4]

In accordance with the strategic planning documents, including the "Strategy of socio-economic development of the Far East and Baikal region for the period through 2025," as well as the development "Strategy of the Arctic zone of the Russian Federation and the national security for the period through 2020," the "Chukotka Autonomous Okrug development strategy through 2030" is designed to achieve a key goal: the increase in income and life quality of the population. This can be achieved by balancing the regional budget.[5]

---

[3] Strategy of socio-economic development of the Far East and the Baikal region for the period through 2025.

[4,6] Strategy of socio-economic development of Chukotka Autonomous Oblast through 2030.

## 2.10.2. ACTION PLANS

The Strategy of socio-economic development of the region through 2030 contains measures of consistent and systematic implementation of the stated priorities:

- Accelerated development of transportation and energy infrastructure by attracting federal funds and conducting extensive geological surveys. This program requires more than 200 billion rubles;
- Attracting private investment for the development of the Baimsky ore zone of the Beringovsky coalfield of up to 150 billion rubles;
- Significantly increasing mining operations done by private companies (growth of industries by 5–6 times);
- Compliance to the instructions of the President of Russia in the development of the social sphere and the corresponding provision of items of expenditure in the regional budget;
- Preservation of national identity, natural and cultural environment, and the habitat of the indigenous peoples of Chukotka.[6]

## 2.10.3. STATE PROGRAMS

The list of Chukotka Autonomous Okrug state programs is shown in Table 2.9.

**TABLE 2.9.**   Chukotka Autonomous Okrug State Programs

| Number | Name of the state program |
|--------|---------------------------|
| 1 | "Development of the health care system in Chukotka Autonomous Okrug for the period from 2014 through 2020" |
| 2 | "Development of the education system, culture and youth policies in Chukotka Autonomous Okrug for the period from 2014 through 2018" |
| 3 | "Social assistance of the population in Chukotka Autonomous Okrug for the period from 2014 through 2018" |
| 4 | "Stimulating economic activity of the population in Chukotka Autonomous Okrug for the period from 2014 through 2018" |

[6] Strategy of socio-economic development of Chukotka Autonomous Oblast through 2030.

**TABLE 2.9.** (Continued).

| Number | Name of the state program |
|---|---|
| 5 | "Development of physical culture, sports and tourism in Chukotka Autonomous Okrug for the period from 2014 through 2018" |
| 6 | "Development of agriculture in Chukotka Autonomous Okrug for the period from 2014 through 2018" |
| 7 | "Information society in Chukotka Autonomous Okrug for the period from 2014 through 2018" |
| 8 | "Housing, utilities and energy assistance in Chukotka Autonomous Okrug for the period from 2014 through 2018" |
| 9 | "Development of infrastructure in Chukotka Autonomous Okrug for the period from 2014 through 2018" |
| 10 | "Development of transportation infrastructure in Chukotka Autonomous Okrug for the period from 2014 through 2018" |
| 11 | "Development of the forest industry in Chukotka Autonomous Okrug for the period from 2014 through 2018" |
| 12 | "Regional finance management in Chukotka Autonomous Okrug for the period from 2014 through 2018" |
| 13 | "Strengthening the unity of the Russian nation, ethno-cultural development of the Russian peoples, and government support to social non-commercial organizations in Chukotka Autonomous Okrug for the period from 2014 through 2020" |
| 14 | "The resettlement of citizens from the residential premises that were recognized as being in a state of emergency in Chukotka Autonomous Okrug for the period from 2014 through 2018" |
| 15 | "Public safety and road safety in Chukotka Autonomous Okrug for the period from 2014 through 2018" |
| 16 | "Protection from natural and man-made disasters and fire protection in Chukotka Autonomous Okrug for the period from 2015 through 2019" |

## 2.10.4. PROJECTS LISTED IN THE STRATEGY AND STATE PROGRAMS

Projects listed in the strategy of the socio-economic development of the Far East and the Baikal region for the period through 2025:

- Creation of a large coal extraction center containing a coil-mining enterprise with production of up to 12 million tons per year and a deep-water berthing facility with a transshipping complex for year-round work on transshipment of coal to heavy-tonnage marine vessels. For the purposes of implementing the investment project, it will be required to build a coal-mining enterprise and a sea port at Beringovsky, as well as to build an overhead power transmission line (110 kW) Anadyr-Beringovsky and a motor way Anadyr – Field Verkhne-Telekaiskoye – Beringovsky;[7]

- It is planned to construct an oil refinery with a capacity of 350,000 tons per year with the appropriate infrastructure including a heated oil pipeline, an originating pump station, a bulk plant, and a new berth in the sea port in Anadyr town;
- The creation of the Chaun-Bilibinskaya zone of advanced economic growth will be carried out by way of developing gold-silver deposits having low and medium reserves with bucked ores both within the boundaries and near the known ore clusters (Kupol, Valunistoye) and in the prospective areas of Verkhne-Yablonevskaya and Kanchalano-Amguemskaya metallogenic zones;
- Transportation systems of the Chukotka Autonomous District opening onto Magadan Oblast and the Republic of Sakha (Yakutia) will be integrated. Development of the internal transportation network of the region will be represented by motor ways Anadyr – Field Verkhne-Telekaiskoye-Beringovsky and Bilibino – Anyuisk, which will enable the creation of an appropriate regional transportation infrastructure, reduce dependence on seasonal cargo delivery, and minimize budget costs;
- Planned construction of the year-round operating seaport in the settlement of Beringovsky will enable dynamic development of the region's coal-mining industry;
- Reconstruction of the airport at Anadyr (Ugolny) will not only provide an opportunity to fully use it for the purposes of air carriages of passengers and cargo on long-haul destinations including international ones, but will also become the basis of regional aviation;
- It is planned to restore navigation on the rivers of the Anadyrsky basin with corresponding navigational and hydrographic support;

---

[7] Strategy of socio-economic development of the Far-East and the Baikal region for the period until 2025.

- In order to ensure the satisfaction of demand for electricity in the self-contained power system of the Chukotka Autonomous District, Egvekinotskaya GRES will be reconstructed, and a nuclear heat and power plant will be constructed on the basis of a floating power unit with reactor facilities KLT-40C in the town of Pevek for the substitution of the thermal power station in Pevek, which exhausted its life span many times;
- Construction of new power lines (110 kW) Komsomolskoye – Maiskoye, Bilibino-Kupol, Kupol-Peschanka and Anadyr-Beringovsky will fully supply the industrial users developing the gold ore fields at Maiskoye, Dvoinoye and Kupol, the Peschanka copper deposits, and the Beringovsky coal basin with electric power. Reconstruction of the existing high voltage power line (110 kW) Bilibino-Komsomolsky-Pevek, the modernization of the electric power system in the town of Pevek, and the installation of a 35 kW emergency cable link based upon the project "Submarine cable duct with voltage of 35 kW through the Anadyr River" will enhance electric reliability for the supplier of Chaun-Bilibinsky and Anadyrsky electrical generation systems. Construction of high voltage power lines (110 kW) Valunistoye – Komsomolsky and Ugolniye Kopi-Kanchalan-Valunistoye will facilitate the connection of three electrical systems and create an opportunity of power exchange between them as well as enhance electric reliability and quality for suppliers.[8]

Items set out in the Strategy of economic and social development of the Chukotka Autonomous District until 2030 are as follows:

- Industrial areas (territories) of advanced development: the Anadyrskaya industrial area and the Chaun-Bilibinskaya industrial area. These areas are divided as follows:
  - The Anadyrskaya industrial area includes development of deposits of hard coal in the Beringovsky coal basin and oil and gas in the Anadyrsky and Khatyrsky petroleum basins. Currently, to meet the domestic needs of the District, the Zapadno-Ozernoye gas field has been put into operation. An investment project for the development

---

[8] Strategy of socio-economic development of the Far-East and the Baikal region for the period until 2025.

of deposits in the Amaamskaya and Verkhne-Alkatvaamskaya areas of the Beringovsky coal basin oriented to high-quality coal exportation to the countries of the Asia-Pacific Region is being prepared;

○ The Chaun-Bilibinskaya industrial area includes development of one of the largest deposits of gold, silver, tin, and copper in Russia. The gold ore fields at Maiskoye, Kupol, Karalveem and Dvoynoye have now been put into operation. The Kekura and Klen gold fields are being prepared for operation in the short term. The long-term strategic outlook is represented by the development of tin fields (Pyrkakaiskiye Stock Works) and the development of fields in the Baimskaya ore zone, and primarily, the Cu-Au porphyry deposit "Peschanka" – the largest deposit of copper in the northeast of Russia.

## 2.11. STRATEGIC OBSERVATIONS

Based on the results of examining the strategies, plans, and programs for social and economic development of the Far Eastern Federal District and its constituent units, the following conclusions may be drawn:

- In many cases, strategies for the development of constituent entities lack plans for their implementation;
- The main items of higher-priority development belong to the oil and gas industry (including the petrochemical industry), transport infrastructure, the electric-power industry, the coal-mining industry, and the fisheries industry.

# CHAPTER 3

# STRATEGIES AND PLANS FOR THE FEDERAL EXECUTIVE POWER AND STATE-OWNED COMPANIES IN THE CONSTITUENT TERRITORIES OF THE RUSSIAN FEDERATION INCLUDED IN THE FAR EASTERN FEDERAL DISTRICT

## 3.1. FEDERAL MINISTRY FOR THE DEVELOPMENT OF THE RUSSIAN PACIFIC COAST REGION

### 3.1.1. "ECONOMIC AND SOCIAL DEVELOPMENT OF THE FAR EAST AND BAIKAL REGIONS FOR THE PERIOD UNTIL 2025" FEDERAL TARGET PROGRAM

In 2014, the Ministry accepted the "Economic and social development of the Far East and Baikal regions for the period until 2025" federal target program, which underlines key projects that would aid the intensive development of the Far Eastern District.[9]

## 3.1.2. TERRITORIES OF PRIORITY DEVELOPMENT

On February 12th 2015, the government sub-commission for the implementation of investment projects in the Far East accepted the first three

[9] http://www.garant.ru/products/ipo/prime/doc/70544078/

territories of developmental priority: Khabarovsk TDP, Komsomolsk TDP and Nadejdinskaya (Primorskii Krai) TDP. In order to create the infrastructure of these TDPs, state funding of 6.2 billion rubles is needed. The required private funding is stated at 50 billion rubles.[10]

### 3.1.3. PRIORITY INVESTMENT PROJECTS

On February 12, 2015, during a hearing in the government sub-commission of investment project implementation in the Far East, the first six planned projects were accepted. The total amount of private investment was numbered at 126.54 billion rubles. The amount of state investment was 16.5 billion rubles.[11]

## 3.2. MINISTRY OF NATURAL RESOURCES AND ENVIRONMENT OF THE RUSSIAN FEDERATION

In 2013 and 2014, with the active participation of the Ministry, a set of laws was adopted that included tax-free dates for the minerals exemption tax (MET) in the Far East for solid minerals, differentiation of the MET rates in the development of stranded oil reserves, and the establishment of a special tax regime for the extraction of hydrocarbons on the continental shelf. In Magadan Oblast, a project draft for the industrial development of Lankovsky and Melkovodninsky lignite deposits in Olsk district is being prepared.

The planned annual production will amount to 2.7 million tons of brown coal. The project cost is more than 15 billion rubles[12]

## 3.3. MINISTRY OF INDUSTRY AND TRADE OF THE RUSSIAN FEDERATION

The largest project supervised by the Ministry in the Far East is the creation of the Far Eastern Shipbuilding and Ship Repair Center with a

---

[10] http://minvostokrazvitia.ru/press-center/news_minvostok/?ELEMENT_ID=2959.
[11] http://minvostokrazvitia.ru/press-center/news_minvostok/?ELEMENT_ID=2959.
[12] http://jp-ru.org/data/tsudai/magadan.pdf.

value of about 112 billion rubles. In addition, the assembly of Japanese and Korean vehicles with the Sollers Company project is being supervised in conjunction with the Ministry of Economic Development of the Russian Federation. Within the framework of the federal target program "Economic and social development of the Far East and the Baikal Region until 2025," the Ministry studies large investment projects in the regions and considers granting TAD (territories with advancing socio-economic development) status to the territories.

## 3.4. MINISTRY OF AGRICULTURE OF THE RUSSIAN FEDERATION

In the Far Eastern Federal District, the Ministry operates under the "State program for the development of agriculture and regulation of agricultural products, raw materials, and food for 2013–2020." One of the objectives of the sub-program is to develop socially important sectors such as sheep and goat breeding, reindeer breeding, and horse breeding to ensure the preservation of the traditional way of life and employment of independent nations, including the peoples of the Far North, Siberia, and the Far East. The total volume of investment is expected to be about 500 billion rubles (see: the text of the "Development of livestock sub-sector, refining and sale of animal products" subprogram).[13]

## 3.5. MINISTRY OF COMMUNICATIONS AND MASS MEDIA OF THE RUSSIAN FEDERATION

The main focus of the Ministry in the Far Eastern Federal District is the development of regional communication links. For example, in the area of Cape Tabaginsky near the Lena River crossing, a Tynda – Yakutsk fiber-optic pillared communication line was launched. The total length of the line is 680 km. The length is 45 km from the area of Lower Best to Yakutsk. The length of the fiber-optical communication line over the river is more than 6 km. In the south of Sakhalin Island, the construction of a

---

[13] http://www.consultant.ru/document/cons_doc_LAW_162737/?frame=2.

Yuzhno – Sakhalinsk – Poronaisk fiber-optic communication line has been completed. Preparatory works are underway on the coastline of the Sea of Okhotsk as part of the Sakhalin – Magadan – Kamchatka underwater fiber-optic communication line project.

## 3.6. MINISTRY OF TRANSPORT OF THE RUSSIAN FEDERATION

The Federal Road Agency (*Rosavtodor*) is conducting a number of large projects in the Far Eastern Federal District. These include construction of the Viluy road in Yakutia with the total initial cost over 3.9 billion rubles, the Kolyma road that will cost more than 3 billion rubles, and the road bridge over Lena river near Yakutsk worth more than 56 billion rubles. The construction of a Blagoveshchensk – Heihe road bridge is under consideration.

## 3.7. MINISTRY OF ECONOMIC DEVELOPMENT OF THE RUSSIAN FEDERATION

The ministry of Economic Development with the Sollers Company intends to increase the production of Toyota, Mazda, SsangYong cars to 125 thousand per year, as well as to increase the level of local production up to 30%. The project implementation period is 2013–2015. The project cost is 24 billion rubles.

## 3.8. VNESHECONOMBANK STATE CORPORATION

Vnesheconombank and the Primorsky Territory Administration approved a joint action plan for the comprehensive development of the Pacific Coast region in 2013–2018. As part of the approved plan, the regional authorities will consider 12 projects, the cost of which total more than 250 billion rubles. Priority will be offered to agriculture, refining of natural resources, industry, and transport infrastructure. The financing of investment projects will be carried out as a public–private partnership (PPP). In Yakutia, the bank participates in the Mechel Group funding of the development of the northwestern section of the Elga coal deposit. In agriculture (with the Summa Corporate Group), the bank is involved in financing the construction of a grain terminal with the capacity to handle up to 11 million tons of grain.

# 3.9. ROSATOM STATE ATOMIC ENERGY CORPORATION

On the territory of the Sakha (Yakutia) Republic, Atomredmetzoloto JSC (belongs to Atomenergoprom JSC) is building the Elkon mining and steel plant. The estimated volume of investment is 90 billion rubles. The project is currently suspended due to the decline in demand for uranium and the termination of a number of programs for the construction of nuclear power plants. With Zoloto Seligdara JSC, the corporation develops gold-uranium deposits in the Aldan district (ZAO Lunnoe). Currently, the state balance received 3 tons of C1 category gold; inferred resources are estimated at 28 tons. The average gold grade is 3.9 g/t, uranium grade is 540 g/t. In Chukotka Autonomous Region, Rosenergoatom JSC will be constructing a floating power block with the capacity of $2 \times 35$ megawatts, costing more than 20 billion rubles, as part of the Chaun-Bilibinsk industrial zone development. Furthermore, in order to replace the currently existing Bilibino NPP, the construction of new power generators is planned. The cost of the project is estimated at 48 billion rubles.

# 3.10. ROSTEC STATE COMPANY

In Amur Oblast, the state company, in conjunction with the world's largest coal company Shenhua, plans for the comprehensive development of the Ogodzhinsky coal deposit with a planned capacity of 30 million tons by 2019. Signed in September 2014, the memorandum underlines not only the coal mining and transportation plans, but also plans involving the construction of thermal power plants and high-voltage transmission lines to export power to China. The volume of planned investments amounts to 10 billion US dollars.[14] In Primorsky Krai, the construction of Port Vera, a coal sea transshipment terminal, is being planned.[15] Under the

---

[14] http://www.kommersant.ru/doc/2559807..
[15] http://rostec.ru/news/4513703.

project framework, the cooperation takes place between the subsidiary of Rostec, "PT – Global Resources," and the world's coal producer, Shenhua. Construction for the Port Vera coal sea transshipment terminal is planned in the vicinity of Mys Otkrytyi, Primorsky Krai, in an ice-free area. The cargo turnover of the port is anticipated to be 20 million tons per year.

In Yakutia, the Vostok Engineering company (a subsidiary of the Triarkmayning company – a joint venture of Rostec and the IST group) won an auction for the right to use a subsoil area of the Tomtor deposit (Byrany area). The tomtor deposit is one of the largest deposits in the world; its area is 250 square km. Reserves are estimated at 154 million tones of ore containing 6.71% niobium oxide, 0.6% of yttrium, 0.048% of scandium and 9.53% of terbium. Investment in the project is estimated at 30 billion rubles during the period of 6 years.[16]

## 3.11. FEDERAL SPECIAL CONSTRUCTION AGENCY (SPETSSTROY)

In the Amur region, the company performs contract work for the construction of the Vostochny Cosmodrome.

## 3.12. RUSSIAN FEDERAL SPACE AGENCY (ROSCOSMOS)

Responsible for the construction of the Vostochny Cosmodrome in Amur Oblast. By 2020, 492 billion rubles (in 2010 prices) will be invested in the construction of a new Russian cosmodrome.

## 3.13. THE FEDERAL AGENCY FOR THE DEVELOPMENT OF THE STATE BORDER FACILITIES OF THE RUSSIAN FEDERATION (ROSGRANITSA)

In the Jewish Autonomous Oblast, the agency conducts renovation of the border area at the Nizhneleninskoye, Amurzet and Pashkovo checkpoints

---

[16] http://rostec.ru/news/3862.

because floods have destroyed most of the coastal area and special facilities.

## 3.14. VNESHTORGBANK (VTB) GROUP

In the transportation sector, the Bank is cooperating with the Government of the Khabarovsk Krai on the construction of the Eastern Bypass of Khabarovsk toll road. The cost of construction is estimated at 16 billion rubles. The Eastern Bypass can start operating in 2017.[17]

## 3.15. UNITED SHIPBUILDING STATE CORPORATION

This corporation's largest project in Primorsky Krai is the construction of the Zvezda shipyard – a modern shipbuilding complex that guarantees the production of tankers of up to 350 thousand tons, liquefied natural gas (LNG) carriers, ice-class vessels, specialized vessels, offshore platforms elements and other types of marine technology. The project implementation period is 2010–2018 and the cost of the project is 111.7 billion rubles.

In Kamchatka Krai, Severo-Vostochnyi Remontniy Center JSC (part of the United Shipbuilding State Corporation) is involved in the wharf modernization project. The cost of work is more than 2 billion rubles. The corporation initiated a discussion regarding the creation of a single center for civil and military shipbuilding and ship repair on the basis of Petropavlovskaya Sudoverf JSC and Severo-Vostochnyi Remontniy Center JSC. The total cost of the project could reach more than 13 billion rubles.

## 3.16. GAZPROM JSC

The Power of Siberia pipeline will go from the Chayandinskoye deposit in Yakutia to Vladivostok via Khabarovsk. The total length of the gas pipeline is about 4,000 km; the length of the "Yakutia – Khabarovsk – Vladivostok"

---

[17] http://www.kommersant.ru/doc/2035558.

section is about 3200 km. The length of the "Irkutsk Oblast – Yakutia" section is about 800 km. The pipeline performance will be over 61 billion cubic meters of gas per year, 38 billion of which will be exported to China for a period of 30 years. Investment in the project will amount to about 1 trillion rubles.

On Sakhalin Island, the construction of a third LNG line with a capacity of up to 5 million tons is planned in the framework of oil and gas for the Sakhalin-2 project. Gazprom is also working on a "Vladivostok LNG" project, which involves the construction of an LNG plant near Vladivostok. The planned capacity of the plant will be no less than 15 million tons of liquefied gas per year. The first line with a capacity of 5 million tons per year is planned for 2018.

## 3.17. RUSHYDRO

In Magadan Oblast, the Ust-Srednekanskaya 570 megawatts hydropower plant has been launched at a cost of more than 42 billion rubles; in Amur Oblast, the Nizhny-Bureysk 320 megawatts hydropower plant worth 37.7 billion rubles has been built. The construction of the Kankun hydropower plant in Yakutia was suspended due to a decrease in the demand for electricity by the mining companies in the region. Construction of the TPP in Yakutsk is near completion. The construction of the 120 megawatts TPSC with a cost of 18.5 billion rubles in the city of Sovetskaya Gavan is underway. The second stage of the 110 megawatts Blagoveshensk TPS is currently under construction.

In Kamchatka Krai, the construction of a hydropower plant system on the Zhupanova River project is being studied. The total capacity of hydropower plants could reach approximately 100 megawatts. The project cost amounts to about 90 billion rubles. In Magadan Oblast, Magadanenergo is constructing an Oratukan-Palatka-Centralnaya electric-power transmission line (VL220), which costs 8.5 billion rubles. It is noteworthy that the project is to build a plant that produces liquefied hydrogen based on the energy from Ust-Srednekanskaya HPP. The project involves the participation of the Federal Hydro Company – RusHydro, Energeticheskiye Sistemy Vostoka JSC and Kawasaki Heavy Industries (Japan).

In South Sakhalin, the first stage of construction is underway for the Sakhalin-2 hydroelectric power station with a capacity of 120 MW and a cost of more than 20 billion rubles. The planned reconstruction of the Yuzhno-Sakhalinsk CHPP-1 will cost more than 24 billion rubles. In the city of Sovetskaya Gavan in Khabarovsk Krai, the TPCS project is designed for a capacity of 120 MW and 200 Gcal/h. The project will cost about 18 billion rubles. The second stage of the scheme for electric power from the CHP in Sovetskaya Gavan is scheduled for January 2015. The project includes the construction of a 110 kV transmission line with a length of 37 kilometers to the village of Vanino and a 13 km line of 110 kV to the town of Okocha. There will also be construction of two distribution substations: one in the Egge Bay area (with a 10/35/110 kV voltage line) and one near the village of Okocha (at 110 kV). In Primorye, RAO ES the East will initiate a project to build Ussuriysk and Nakhodka CHP. In 2012, a strategic cooperation agreement on the construction of the Ussuri TPCS was signed between RAO ES the East, Bank of China, and the Heilongjiang Engineering Alliance, called the "Amur Energo-Story Alliance." China is ready to invest in the construction of the thermal power station in exchange for electricity.

The power of each TPP will amount to 370 MW. It is planned that the Ussuri TPCS will operate on coal and Nakhodka TPCS on gas. For the period until 2018, 108 billion rubles is needed.

## 3.18. FSK EES

In Amur Oblast, the construction of the VL500 Zeya HPP – Amurskaya Substation – China transmission line, worth more than 5 billion rubles, is underway. The construction of a Fevralsk – Rydnaya electric-power transmission line (VL220) is viewed as a potential project.

## 3.19. ROSNEFT

In Primorsky Krai, the company began to implement the investment project for the construction of the Eastern Petrochemical Complex (EPC) with a capacity of up to 30 million tons of hydrocarbon raw materials in the city of Nakhodka. The preliminary cost of the project is estimated at 1.3 trillion rubles. The term of the project (stage 3) will run until 2028.

In Khabarovsk Krai, Rosneft plans to build a new oil line of 350 km from the Eastern Siberia – Pacific Ocean system to the Rosneft plant (refinery) in Komsomolsk-on-Amur that will cost more than 48 billion rubles. A project for the construction of a deep refining complex at the LLC RN-Komsomolsk Oil Refining Plant with a capacity of 1 million tons of tar, 2 million tons of hydrocracking, and 3.6 million tons of raw materials per year. The cost of this project is more than 57 billion rubles. The company has plans to build an oil and oil products export terminal at the port of De-Kastri with the possibility of handling 5 million tons and with an investment value of 10.5 billion rubles. In Magadan Oblast, the company is developing a project for the extraction of oil and gas on the shelf of the Sea of Okhotsk (the participants are Kashevarovsky, Lisyanskii, and Magadan-1,2,3). The cost of the project is more than 46 billion rubles with an implementation period from 2014 to 2025 (see: Catalog of Investment Projects in Magadan Oblast).

Magadanmorneftegaz (Rosneft) is studying the possibility of building an additional deep-water wharf (behind Wharf No.6 and Wharf No.7) in Magadan. On Sakhalin Island, in 2018, Rosneft plans to build a plant to produce LNG at a capacity of up to 10 million tons. The resource base for the plant will be the Sakhalin (the Sakhalin-3 project), Yakutsk, and Irkutsk gas production centers. Anticipated investment could reach 8 billion US dollars.

## 3.20. RUSSIAN RAILWAYS (RZD)

The largest project of Russian Railways in the Far Eastern Federal District will be the development and modernization of Baikal-Amur Mainline (BAM-2), which will cost about 560 billion rubles. In addition, the construction project of the railway line Berkakit – Tomot – Yakutsk, stretching over 800 km and costing more than 40 billion rubles, has been completed.

## 3.21. SUKHOI COMPANY

In Komsomolsk-on-Amur, the company provides technical retooling and modernization of the Komsomolsk-on-Amur Aircraft Production Association manufacturer. The cost of the project exceeds 26 billion rubles.

## 3.22. ALROSA OJSC

In 2014, the company commissioned the Udachny underground diamond mine. Upon reaching the projected capacity, the mine will be able to extract more than 5 million carats of diamonds per year.

## 3.23. FUND FOR THE DEVELOPMENT OF THE FAR EAST AND THE BAIKAL REGION JSC

Fund for the Development of the Far East and the Baikal region JSC is conducting a number of projects in the Far Eastern Federal District.

The construction of the railway bridge over Amur River from Nizhneleninskoye (RF) to Tuntsyan (China) is planned on the Russia-China border in Jewish Autonomous Oblast. The project has strategic importance for the macro-regional economy because it will allow the introduction of a systemic incentive to develop new export-oriented manufacturing in the FEFD, as well as the creation of a logistics and industrial cluster in Jewish Autonomous Oblast. The capacity of the bridge will amount to 5.2 million tons with a projected increase to 20 million tons.

The Fund is looking into the possibility of merging with the companies that own Vladivostok International Airport to further promote the development of the hub. The Singaporean operator Changi Airports International, an international company with vast experience in implementing traffic networks and operating and maintaining the largest foreign airline hubs, acts as the Fund's partner. The necessity to develop the airport is due to the forthcoming increase in passenger and cargo flows following the construction of new regional production facilities, the expansion of automobile production, the development of seaports, and the creation of the Primorye integrated entertainment zone.

Together with the Government of Primorsky Krai, the Fund finances the construction of the Vladivostok – Nakhodka – Vostochny port road. The projected road is a key element in the Primorye-1 international transportation network. The usage of concession mechanisms is intended in the implementation of this project. The construction of the road is aimed at the development of the Vostochny Port – Nakhodka – Vladivostok – Ussuriysk – Pogranichny international transportation network that will tie together the main Primorsky Krai seaports with northeastern Chinese provinces and will allow access to the FEFD infrastructure. Moreover, one of the road sections will tie together the Vladivostok International Airport with the Primorye integrated entertainment zone. Currently, the construction of the first stage is underway. The project's cost is 7.1 billion rubles[18]; completion of the project is scheduled for the first quarter of 2016. The cost of construction during the second stage will be 22.9 billion rubles.

In Sakhalin Oblast, the creation of a fishing industry cluster based on the partnership with Sapsan Group is planned. On Shikotan Island, the expansion and modernization of the production sphere is planned with the construction of modern facilities for production, storage, and processing of seafood, production of canned fish, and supporting infrastructure. An integrated approach will improve fish extraction and processing efficiency and will bolster the output by 1.5–2 times, as well as increase the product line.

In Yakutia, with the participation of the Government of the Sakha (Yakutia) Republic, South Yakutia Development Corporation JSC is building a power grid infrastructure to provide an external power supply to the Inaglinsky Coal Complex. The Fund intends to participate in the construction of substations (110 kV) and high voltage lines (110 kV) with a length of 7.5 km for the external energy supply of the Inaglinsky Coal Complex. Since 2011, the Kolmar Coal Complex in the "Integrated development of South Yakutia" framework is building the Inaglinsky Coal Complex, which has an annual output of 2 million tons of coke gas concentrate (with the prospect of increased output), with their own and raised funds. The

---

[18]http://vestiprim.ru/2014/06/03/v-primore-sproektirovan-vtoroy-etap-stroitelstva-dorogi-vladivo-stok-nahodka-port-vostochnyy.html

main constraint is a lack of external power supply that would provide the Inaglinsky Coal Complex with the necessary power. The construction of the electricity system infrastructure project will be implemented via concession mechanism (Federal Law 115 "On Concession Agreements").

## 3.24. OJSC ROSTELECOM

The OJSC Rostelecom *Far East* Macroregion branch operates in the FEFD, with offices located all over the region. Presently, the company has completed reparatory work on the Sea of Okhotsk's coastline as part of the Sakhalin – Magadan – Kamchatka underwater fiber-optic communication line project. This new line will connect the city of Okha on the Sakhalin Island with Magadan Oblast and Kamchatka Krai. The fiber-optic communication line will be layered on the bottom of the Sea of Okhotsk. The length of the communication line will be 2000 km with the system's capacity being 400 Gb per second in each direction (with the possibility of increasing the capacity up to 8 Tb per second). In 2015, the fiber-optic communication line will be complete. The operation is scheduled to start in June 2016.

## 3.25. JSC INTER RAO UES

In Amur Oblast, the company is planning the construction of the Erkovetsk power plant. This TPCS will allow the export of 30–50 billion kW/hour per year to China – up to 5% of all Russian electric energy output. The cost of the project will be 14–26 billion US dollars, including the construction of the EPT line.[19] In Khabarovsk Krai, the construction of the energy bridge Khabarovsk Krai – Sakhalin – Japan, with a total generating capacity of up to 3 GW in three stages, is under consideration. The first and second stages focus on constructing the coal-fired power plants on Sakhalin Island. These power plants will generate 350 MW each. The third stage is the construction of the gas power plant, consisting of 2 blocks of 400 MW each. To transport electric energy from Russia, a combination of overhead EPT lines on both Russian and Japanese territory might be used. In addition, an underwater DC cable might be used to

[19] http://www.kommersant.ru/doc/2405853.

transport electric energy from Sakhalin Island to Hokkaido Island. In the long term (the third stage), two underwater Mainland – Sakhalin Island DC cables of 500 kW each, are planned to be installed in order to export more energy from the UES of the East. The financing is planned to come from several parties: 50% of state funds, 30% of borrowed funds, and 20% of the company's funds.[20]

In Sakhalin Oblast, the reconstruction of the Nogliksk gas power plant is under consideration.

The initiator is OJSC Nogliksk Gas Power Station. The installed capacity of the plant can be increased from 48 MW to 84 MW, taking into account the long-term development of the Nogliksk District and the northern Sakhalin. Three recovery boilers are set to use the heat from the exhausted gas of power generating units in order to improve the efficiency of the station. The cost of the work will be more than 7 billion rubles. [21]

# 3.26. SBERBANK

In the Amur region, Sberbank together with Amur Agro Holding is funding the creation of a soy industry cluster. It is expected that the company will produce up to 50 thousand tons of high quality soybean seeds per year. The approximate cost of the first stage will amount to 1.5 billion rubles. In addition, Sberbank plans to participate in the development of Kamchatka Krai based on the cooperation agreement between the bank and the Government of the Kamchatka Krai. This involves cooperation in the development of infrastructure, the tourism industry, the fishing industry, the agriculture and food industry, and the mineral and energy complex.[22] In the southern Sakhalin, the Bank is going to support a number of investment projects to be implemented in Sakhalin Oblast by 2025. These include the construction of kindergartens, as well as the participation in the new Kuril Islands development program.[23]

---

[20] http://www.kommersant.ru/pda/kommersant.html?id=1605550.
[21] http://skr.su/news/233254.
[22] http://www.sberbank.ru/moscow/ru/press_center/all/index.php?id114=200004665.
[23] http://amurmedia.ru/news/economics/19.03.2014/343783/sberbank-podderzhit-investitsionnie-proekti-sahalinskoy-oblasti.html.

## 3.27. TRANSNEFT JSC

The largest project in the Far East is the exploitation of the Eastern Siberia – Pacific Ocean (ESPO) pipeline and the expansion of its capacity to up to 80 million tons per year. The participants of the project are the Kozmino oil port and Transneft-Logistics railway company, which owns 1000 railroad cars and delivers oil from Skovorodino to Kozmino and to an enterprise in Amur Oblast.

## 3.28. ROSVERTOL

In the first quarter of 2015, the Government of Sakhalin Oblast will receive two Mi-8 MTV-1 helicopters from Rosvertol Holding.[24] The use of these new helicopters will increase the number and locations of flights in the region. It will also increase medical aviation capability in the region.

## 3.29. OJSC AEROFLOT – RUSSIAN AIRLINES

OJSC Aeroflot – Russian Airlines participates in subsidized air travel from the Far East, which ensures the availability of air transport for passengers from the region. In 2015, the use of more that 3.372 billion rubles for an air transportation program for passengers from the Far East to the European part of Russia was approved. Aurora airlines (one of Aeroflot's subsidiaries) is the key company in the FEFD. Its business plan aims for a significant increase in the volume of operation. From 2013 to 2018 the number of flights should increase from 172 to 534, and the number of destinations from 30 to 128. During this period, annual flights will reach 2.4 million passengers. By 2018, the total number of the fleet must increase to 40 planes.[25] The airline will connect Vladivostok with cities in the Far East and Siberia, as well as with 40 settlements in Primorsky Krai. In addition to the ten existing airports in Plastun, Kavalerovo, Ternei, Amgu, Maksimovsk,

---

[24] http://amurmedia.ru/news/economics/19.03.2014/343783/sberbank-podderzhit-investitsionnie-proekti-sahalinskoy-oblasti.html 26 http://rostec.ru/news/3967,
[25] http://www.finam.ru/analysis/newsitem79A43/,

Ust-Sobolevka, Svetlaya, Edinka, Samarga and Agzu, there will be another 30 new airports in 15 municipality districts and five city districts.[26]

## 3.30. OJSC TRANSAERO AIRLINES

OJSC Transaero Airlines participates in subsidized air travel from the Far East program, which ensures the availability of air transport to passengers from the region.[27]

## 3.31. STRATEGIC OBSERVATIONS

Based on plans issued by the Federal Government and state companies that concentrate on the FEFD, it is evident that many of them have priority development projects in the Far East.

---

[26]http://www.flyaurora.ru/promo/?&utm_source=adfox&utm_medium=banner&utm_campaign=324271,908271,
[27] http://itar-tass.com/ekonomika/1445032,

# CHAPTER 4

# STRATEGIC PRIORITY DEVELOPMENT INDUSTRIES IN THE FAR EASTERN FEDERAL DISTRICT

Fields in this section were selected in consideration of national interests, priorities and competitive position, and resources endowment.

## 4.1. MINING OF MINERAL RESOURCES

The Far Eastern Federal District ranks first in terms of its volume of mineral resources. There are considerable reserves of diamonds, gold, coal, iron ore, and complex ores concentrated in the territory of the district. There are also reserves of nonmetallic feed.

Oil and gas extraction on the shelf of the Sea of Okhotsk may push the region to development. Inferred resources of raw hydrocarbons make up 40% of total known reserves of Russia. The economy of the northern Far Eastern Federal District (the Sakha (Yakutia) Republic) is generally based on the development of diamond deposits (Aikhal, Mir, Udachnoye), which make up 80% of Russian diamond deposits, as well as gold ore and placer deposits concentrated in Yakutia, Amur and Magadan Oblast, Khabarovsk Krai, and Kamchatka.

Table 4.1 shows that, in terms of the structure of extracted minerals, the Far Eastern Federal District is in a much better position than the Russian Federation as a whole. This is because the diversification of fields by resource categories is notably higher in this region, which thus indicates the comparatively low dependence of the regional economy on the extraction of exhaustible energy resources.

**TABLE 4.1.** The Volume Structure of Goods and Services Shipped, Based on "Extracted Minerals" Economic Activity in 2012[28] (Percentages Based on Actual Prices)

| | | Type of Activity | |
| --- | --- | --- | --- |
| Regions | Total Extracted Minerals | Energy Producing Minerals | Minerals, Excluding Energy Producing Minerals |
| Russian Federation | 100 | 88.5 | 11.5 |
| Far Eastern Federal District | 100 | 64.1 | 35.9 |
| The Sakha (Yakutia) Republic | 100 | 40.3 | 59.7 |
| Kamchatka Krai | 100 | 26.0 | 74.0 |
| Primorsky Krai | 100 | 35.7 | 64.3 |
| Khabarovsk Krai | 100 | 18.5 | 81.5 |
| Amur Oblast | 100 | 3.5 | 96.5 |
| Magadan Oblast | 100 | 1.3 | 98.7 |
| Sakhalin Oblast | 100 | 99.8 | 0.2 |
| Jewish Autonomous Oblast | 100 | 0.5 | 99.5 |
| Chukotka Autonomous Okrug | 100 | 2.0 | 98.0 |

It should be noted, however, that the efficiency of assets exploitation by the enterprises of the region is extremely diverse. Given the relatively high profitability ratio of enterprises in extractive industries (13.3% in the Far Eastern Federal District compared to 11.9% in the Russian Federation), this ratio is considerably lower than the Russian average in the manufacturing industries and real sectors (0.4% versus 8.1% in the manufacturing industries, and in the real sector and distribution of electricity, gas, and water, the region shows complete unprofitability in terms of this ratio – 0.4% versus 0.9% of the national average).

## 4.1.1. COAL

In the production structure of the Far Eastern Federal District's economy, it is necessary to emphasize the coal industry of Yakutia, Primorsky Krai, Sakhalin, Amur and Magadan Oblast. The reserves of hard and pitch

[28] Here and in all further 2012 data percentages are based on actual prices.

coal are concentrated here. This coal is exported to Japan, South Korea, China and other countries of Asia-Pacific Region. The Far Eastern Federal District ranks second in Russia by reserves and extraction of coal. Coal reserves are generally concentrated in the territory of Yakutia (47.5%) and Amur Oblast. Total reserves of pitch coal comprise 61%; of this hard coals amounts to 38.9% and soldering coals to 20%.

Along with those operated in the territory of the Far Eastern Federal District, there are a number of promising deposits that have not faced commercial development yet. Among these are the Elginsky deposit in Yakutia with reserves of soldering coal amounting to 2.2 billion tons, and areas of the Chulmakansky and Denisovsky coal deposit with reserves of more than 1 billion tons; the Ogodzhinsky deposit of hard coal and Sergeevsky deposit of pitch coal in Amur Oblast are being developed; projects on the development of coal chemistry in Magadan Oblast on the basis of the Lankovsky and Melkovodnensky deposits of pitch coal with reserves of more than 1.6 billion tons are under consideration. The Yuzhno-Omolonsky deposit in Magadan Oblast with expected reserves of more than 440 tons of soldering coals was explored. The development of coal deposits in Sakhalin is being continued. The extraction increase is to be achieved by developing the Solntsevsky deposit on the subsurface resources site, Yuzhny, and a mine, Udarnovskaya. Noteworthy is the project of development on the Beringovsky coal deposit in the Anadyrsky District of Chukotka with reserves of more than 4 billion tons and the prospect of exporting products to the countries of Southeast Asia.

## 4.1.2. OIL AND NATURAL GAS

The Far Eastern Federal District is the fourth largest producer of oil among Russian federal districts, and the second largest producer of natural gas. The main reserves of oil and gas are located in the territory of Yakutia and Sakhalin. The Chayandinsky oil and gas condensate deposit is the base and the development of this is expected to start a gas production center in Yakutia. The project is being carried out simultaneously with construction of a gas pipeline, the Power of Siberia, with a capacity of more than 61 billion cubic meters of gas annually, and the export to China will amount to approximately 38 billion cubic meters out of this figure. In addition, it is planned to develop gas condensate deposits Sredne-Tyunskoye and Otradninsky in Lensky district with known reserves of more than 200 billion cubic meters and a gas condensate deposit in Kisil-Sir with reserves up to 400 billion cubic meters. The commercial development of the Zapadno-Anabarsky licensed subsurface resource site in the territory of the Sakha (Yakutia) Republic with oil reserves of up to 12 million tons and natural gas reserves of up to 10 billion cubic meters is possible.

An oil and gas project, named Sakhalin-1, involves the development of oil and gas reserves on the northeastern shelf of Sakhalin Island. The volume of recoverable reserves is estimated at 307 million tons of oil and 485 billion cubic meters of natural gas. An oil-and-gas project, Sakhalin-2, includes two deposits: Piltun-Astokhskoye and Lunskoye. The recoverable reserves amount to 174 million tons of oil and 635 billion cubic meters of natural gas. A project, Sakhalin-3, includes four blocks of deposits: Kirinsky, Veninsky, Aiashsky, and Vostochno-Odoptinsky on the shelf of the Sea of Okhotsk. The reserves of recoverable resources exceed 700 million tons of oil and 1.3 billion cubic meters of natural gas. Products will be exported to the countries of the Asia-Pacific Region.

## 4.1.3. GOLD

The Far Eastern Federal District ranks second (33.3%) in terms of total known reserves of gold and ranks first in terms of gold extraction (53.1%) among all federal districts of Russia. There are 3659 gold deposits in the territory of the district including 107 primary deposits, 3539 placer deposits, and 13 integrated deposits. The majority of deposits are concentrated in Magan Oblast (1182) and the Sakha (Yakutia) Republic (781), in Amur Oblast (614), in Chukotka (531), and in Khabarovsk Krai (373). The Selemdginskaya subzone in Amur Oblast with total reserves of more than 60 tons may be considered to be promising in terms of development and extraction.

**TABLE 4.2.** Minerals in FEFD

| Minerals | Coal (in million of tons) | Oil (in million of tons) | Natural Gas (in billion of cubic meters) | Gold (in tons) | Platinum (in tons) | Iron Ore (in million of tons) |
|---|---|---|---|---|---|---|
| Total (World) | 4700.00 | 4133.0 | 3477.00 | 3109.00 | >180 | 3000.00 |
| Total (Russia) | 352.00 | 523.00 | 669.00 | 272.00 | 26.00 | 100.00 |
| FEFD | 35.04 | 20.89 | 29.76 | 109.00 | 4.40 | ~1 |
| The Sakha (Yakutia) Republic | 12.00 | 5.60 | 1.98 | 22.30 | 0.00 | 0.00 |
| Kamchatka Krai | 0.00 | 0.00 | 0.00 | 0.00 | >0.6 | 0.00 |
| Primorsky Krai | 9.00 | 0.00 | 0.00 | 0.00 | 0.00 | 0.00 |
| Khabarovsk Krai | 5.00 | 0.00 | 0.00 | 20.70 | >3.7 | 0.00 |
| Sakhalin Oblast | 4.00 | 15.30 | 27.50 | 0.00 | 0.00 | 0.00 |
| Magadan Oblast | ~1 | 0.00 | 0.00 | 20.00 | 0.00 | 0.00 |
| Amur Oblast | 3.30 | 0.00 | 0.00 | 28.00 | 0.00 | ~1 |
| Jewish Autonomous Oblast | 0.00 | 0.00 | 0.00 | 0.00 | 0.00 | 0.00 |
| Chukotka Autonomous Okrug | ~1 | 0.00 | ≤0.2 | 18.00 | 0.00 | 0.00 |

**TABLE 4.2.** (Continued).

| Lead Ore (in thousand tons) | Zinc Ore (in thousand tons) | Tin (in tons) | Uranium Ore (in tons) | Diamonds (in million carats) | Fertilizers (in million of tons) | Minerals |
|---|---|---|---|---|---|---|
| > 4000 | 12600.00 | 308600.00 | 53000.00 | >124 | 182.70 | Total (World) |
| 110.90 | 358.50 | 300.00 | 2993.00 | 37.90 | ~19 | Total (Russia) |
| 13.74 | 19.93 | 300.00 | Unavailable | 36.90 | Unavailable | FEFD |
| 0.0 | 0.00 | Unavailable | 0.00 | 36.90 | 0.00 | The Sakha (Yakutia) Republic |
| 0.0 | 0.00 | Unavailable | 0.00 | 0.00 | 0.00 | Kamchatka Krai |
| >10 | 18.40 | Unavailable | 0.00 | 0.00 | 0.00 | Primorsky Krai |
| 0.0 | 0.00 | 300.00 | 0.00 | 0.00 | 0.00 | Khabarovsk Krai |
| 0.0 | 0.00 | Unavailable | 0.00 | 0.00 | 0.00 | Sakhalin Oblast |
| 3.64 | 1.50 | Unavailable | 0.00 | 0.00 | 0.00 | Magadan Oblast |
| 0.0 | 0.00 | Unavailable | 0.00 | 0.00 | 0.00 | Amur Oblast |
| 0.0 | 0.00 | Unavailable | 0.00 | 0.00 | Unavailable | Jewish Autonomous Oblast |
| 0.0 | 0.00 | Unavailable | 0.00 | 0.00 | 0.00 | Chukotka Autonomous Okrug |

The largest project in Magadan Oblast is the development of the Yano-Kolymskaya zone, which includes the Natalkinsky deposit with total reserves of 1449 tons. There are also works being conducted for the development of the Yuzhno-Omolonsky deposit with reserves of approximately 650 tons and the Evensky deposit with 290 tons of gold. The Nezhdaninskoye gold deposit, located in Yakutia and having reserves of approximately 680 tons, can provide for extraction of more than 8 tons of gold annually. More than 11 gold ore facilities with total reserve base of more than 440 tons are developed in Kamchatka. The development of the Chaun-Bilibinskaya industrial area with total reserves of no less than 500 tons holds promise in Chukotka Autonomous Okrug.

## 4.1.4. PLATINUM

Inferred resources of platinum group metals in the Far Eastern Federal District make up 20% of the Russian average and are related to the deposits of Khabarovsk Krai (Konder) and Koryakiya (Galmoenan). The exhaustion of existing reserves is expected to happen in 3–5 years. Among the promising explored deposits is Uorgalan, located 45 km away from Kondera, which has proven reserves of more than 15 tons.

## 4.1.5. IRON ORE

Russia ranks first in the world in terms of known reserves of iron ores. In the Far Eastern Federal District, there is only the Okleminsky deposit in Amur Oblast where ores are extracted (see Table 4.1). Rapid growth is now common to the mining and metallurgical cluster of the Amur River region, which is referred to as the Selemdginskaya subzone and includes the Olekminsky deposit of iron ores (already in operation) with extraction volumes of 2.5 million tons of ore annually; the Garinsky deposit with planned extraction of up to 10 million tons of ore annually; and the Kimkano-Sutarsky deposit in Jewish Autonomous Oblast with planned extraction of approximately 10.5 million tons of ore annually (its operation will commence in 2015). It is planned to export the major part of the output to China. The Yuzhno-Khigansky deposit of ferriferous manganese ores in Jewish Autonomous Oblast with a production capacity of up to 300 thousand tons of ore annually is being developed. A deposit of iron ores in Tayozhnoye, with an estimated capacity of 4 million tons of concentrate annually, is best prepared for commercial development in the Sakha (Yakutia) Republic. The project for development of the Tarynnakhskoye and Gortitskoye iron ore deposits, with the possibility of processing 46 billion tons of ore and an output of 14.6 billion tons of concentrate annually, is also under consideration.

## 4.1.6. LEAD, ZINC, TIN AND RARE EARTH METALS

According to the information available, the inferred resources of lead and zinc in the Far Eastern Federal District make up 27.4% and 15.9% respectively of the Russian average. The extraction of these minerals makes up approximately 70% and 16% (see Table 4.1). Virtually the entire mineral raw material base of tin (100% of resources and more than 95% of reserves) and the whole extraction of it are concentrated in the Far Eastern Federal District. The following are tin deposits in the District: the Deputatskoye deposit in Yakutia (extraction has ceased), the Nevskoye and Iultinskoye deposits in Chukotka Autonomous Okrug, the Khrustalnenskoye and Lifudzinskoye deposits in Primorsky Krai, and the Solnechnoye, Festivalnoye, Khiganskoye deposits in Khabarovsk Krai. The development of the Pravourmiyskoye tin deposit in the Verkhnebureinsky district of Khabarovsk Krai with the possibility of extracting 400 thousand tons of ore and an output of up to 3000 tons of tin annually is probable. Considerable reserves of tin (more than 500 thousand tons) were detected in the Chaun-Bilibinskaya industrial area in Chukotka. The extraction of tin now only occurs in Khabarovsk Krai, given that the volumes of extraction decreased tenfold over the last years; market research has showed more recently, however, both a stable demand for and the price increase of this metal.

Virtually the entire volume of zinc and lead is produced in Primorsky Krai in the territory of the Dalnegorsky ore field. The Cheremshansky ore cluster, which includes the Maiminovskoye deposit, may be of particular interest. The inferred resources of this area are estimated at 26 billion tons of lead-zinc-silver ores. There is also an explored lead-zinc deposit at Verkhnee-Menkechenskoye in Yakutia, which will enable extraction of 65 tons of silver, 8 tons of lead, and 8.5 tons of zinc annually.

The development of a deposit in the Yuzhno-Omolonsky district of Magadan Oblast with expected reserves of 4 million tons of copper, 300 thousand tons of molybdenum, 6.9 million tons of lead, 12.6 million tons of zinc, 760 million tons of iron, and 5 thousand tons of uranium is noteworthy.

Of great interest is the Tomtorskoye deposit of rare earth metals located in Yakutia, 400 km south of the coast of the Laptev Sea. The practical relevance of the deposit is determined by the composition, immense reserves, and unique concentrations of neodymium, yttrium, scandium, and terbium (the "rare earth elements"). The volume of amenable irons in the Buranny area calculated in accordance with the cut-off grade of 1% of $Nb205$ amounts to 42.7 million tons. The reserves of new geological commercial type by category B+C, which means that it is meant for open processing in accordance with the cut-off grade of 3.5% of $Nb205$ and a marginal coefficient of 3.5 m/cubic meters of mining access, in the volume of approximately 1.2 million tons were included in the State balance sheet. This surpasses all analogs known in the world in terms of the reserves and concentrations of $Nb 205$ and $TR203$ and is, thus, unique.

## 4.1.7. URANIUM ORE

Uranium ore is not extracted in the Far Eastern Federal District yet, but in the Sakha (Yakutia) Republic there is the Elkonskoye deposit, which is the largest deposit of uranium ores in the world with reserves of about 600 thousand tons.

## 4.1.8. DIAMONDS

In the Far Eastern Federal District, 80% of the reserves and more than 99% of Russian diamond mining are concentrated in the Sakha (Yakutia)

Republic (see Table 4.2). The further mining of diamonds in the Republic is related to the development of new deposits in Nyurbinsky Ulus. Currently, the total diamond reserves endowment is 35–40 years according to different estimates.

## 4.1.9. MINERAL FERTILIZERS

For the most developed mineral fertilizer deposit in the District, one can refer to the Evgenievskoye deposit of apatites with inferred resources of phosphoric oxide in the amount of 12.5 million tons. Extraction on the deposit has not yet begun. Besides the Evgenievskoye deposit, the developed Seligdarskoye deposit of apatites in Yakutia has the possibility to produce more than 3 million tons of apatite concentrate and 567 thousand tons of mineral fertilizers.

However, there are a number of resources-related limitations that significantly decrease the region's economic growth potential. The main factors that are to be pointed out are as follows:

- Shortage of labor force;
- Remoteness and problems related with vehicle access to mineral bedding and extraction areas;
- Harsh climate conditions;
- Limitation of funds available for investment.

## 4.2. FISHERY COMPLEX

The constituent entities of the Far Eastern Federal District with access to the sea and a significant extent of the coastline have a high potential to develop aquatic resources and are the support for the Russian fishery complex's development.

According to 2013 data, the contribution made by Far Eastern enterprises makes up 70% of all harvesting in the country. The competitive advantage of the region is that it is the best raw materials base among all regions in Russia. It is distinguished by the closeness of the main fishing areas to fleet homeports and processing enterprises, and has diverse aquatic species including those that are the most nutritionally valuable. The world's largest stocks of salmonid fishes (chum salmon, red salmon, spring salmon) as well as red cod (codfish, Pollack, navaga, hake) are in the seas of the Pacific Ocean adjacent to the Far Eastern District; sea dogs, walruses, and seals live there as well. The exclusive economic zone comprises more than 2000 species of various hydrobionts. Today, Russian fishermen, in contrast with Japanese, Chinese, and Korean fisherman, use only several dozens of these species. From the Russian average, 99% of all salmonids, 100% of crabs, over 90% of flounders, more than 40% of herring, approximately 60% of scallops, and approximately 90% of algae are caught in the Pacific Coast basin.[29]

Based on forecasts[30], by 2020 it is planned to introduce about 50% of the total Russian fish-processing capacity for exploitation where more than 60% are for canning capacities and 20% are for refrigerating capacities. It is expected to develop pasturable and marketable fishery in the Far East, which will provide for reconstruction of the existing salmon-fish farms with the promising trend of breeding aquatic biological resources. This is fostered by environmental and hydrological conditions of coastal waters. In this case, fish-breeding development is expected to be innovation-based with efficient use of Russian and foreign research and technologies as well as the best practices. As a result of measures taken to develop the field, the full and efficient development of primary resources reserved to Russia in the exclusive economic zone and coastal waters will be achieved (by no less than 85% until 2020). This will erase the imbalance between the volumes of permissible catch in the exclusive Russian economic zone and production capacities for harvesting, processing, and transportation of aquatic biological resources.

Statistics for the fishery complex in 2013 are as follows:

- Fish catch worldwide – 160 million tons;[31]
- Fish catch in Russia – 4.1 million tons;[32]
- Fish catch in the Far Eastern Federal District – 2.8 million tons;
- Fish catch in Kamchatka Krai – 874 thousand tons;[33]

---

[29] http://biofile.ru/geo/7387.html
[30] http://gossmi.ru/page/gos1_749.htm
[31] http://fish.gov.ru/presscentre/news/Pages/019491.aspx
[32] http://www.vestifinance.ru/articles/37552
[33] http://www.kamchatka.gov.ru/?cont=oiv_din&mcont=5359&menu=4&menu2=0&id=169

- Fish catch in Magadan Oblast – 91 thousand tons;[34]
- Fish catch in Primorsky Krai – 798 thousand tons;[35]
- Fish catch in the Sakha (Yakutia) Republic – 1.25 thousand tons;[36]
- Fish catch in Sakhalin Oblast – 800 thousand tons;[37]
- Fish catch in Khabarovsk Krai – 230 thousand tons;[38]
- Fish catch in Chukotka Autonomous Okrug – 23.4 thousand tons.[39]

In 2013, export of fish and seafood in the Far East made up 1.3 million tons.[40] In the case of an increase in fish catch and the reduction of customs duties for the main species of exported fish, it will be possible to forecast its stable growth.[41]

In view of the data provided, it is possible to draw the following conclusion: the Far Eastern Federal District's fishery complex is its competitive advantage in the field. The basic facilities of the District's fishery complex, which determine its competitive abilities, are concentrated in Kamchatka Krai, Sakhalin Oblast, Primorsky, and Khabarovsk Krai.

## 4.3. FOREST INDUSTRY

Whereas the significant stock of timber is located in the Far Eastern Federal District, the output of timber products is critically low. The field is oriented to transporting unprocessed timber to other regions and exportation. Small outputs of sawn timber, paper, plywood, and pressed wood-fiber board exist in Yakutia, Khabarovsk Krai, Primorsky Krai, and Amur Oblast. Particularly, the total production of timber made up 9% of the Russian average (1.9 million cubic meters) and less than 0.01 % of glued wood, though timber stocks make up about 35% of the Russian average. Nevertheless, enterprises in the regions are functioning successfully.

---

[34] http://www.magadan.ru/ru/government/power/governor/speech/1393208114077.html?printVersion=true
[35] http://www.ya-fermer.ru/news/v-primorskom-krae-bolee-chem-v-15-raza-uvelichilsya-vylov-nekvotiruemyh-obektov-promysla
[36] http://sakha.gov.ru/node/127121
[37] http://yuzhno-sakhalinsk.fishretail.ru/news/sahalinskaya-oblast-ulovi-morskih-bioresursov-v-316066
[38] http://habrus.ru/node/24701
[39] http://anadyr.fishretail.ru/news/itogi-ribohozyaystvennogo-kompleksa-v-2013-godu-podveli-na-chukotke-320756
[40] http://mltrans.ru/news/v-2013-godu-vyros-eksport-ryby-na-dalnem-vostoke/
[41] http://top.rbc.ru/economics/04/08/2014/940747.shtml

More than 600,000 cubic meters of timber (more than 3 million cubic meters during the Soviet period) is harvested in the Sakha (Yakutia) Republic. The production of panel boards with the modern technology MHM, developed in Germany, is especially noteworthy. The prime cost of houses constructed with these boards does not exceed 300,000 rubles per square meter. A whole residential complex of such houses was constructed in Taimyr. Taking into account an extensive area of Yakutia and the scatter of small settlements (amounting to more than 400), the organization of small timber processing complexes, especially with the possibility of added-value wood processing and the utilization of waste products for the power and heat supply of such settlements, is essential and economically advantageous.

Timber-processing enterprises in Khabarovsk Krai have significant growth prospects. It is planned to establish additional sawn timber production units with a production capacity of more than 200,000 cubic meters annually and an output of MDF boards of up to 50,000 cubic meters annually. A portion of these products may be exported to Japan and China.

The project to create a timber-processing complex for added-value wood processing in the Selemdginsky district of Amur Oblast is under consideration. Despite the low stocks of timber in Jewish Autonomous Oblast, timber-processing enterprises are being successfully developed there with the help of Chinese investors. The Pashkovsky timber-processing complex can produce up to 400 thousand cubic meters of timber annually, and the output of sawn timber (120,000 cubic meters), plywood (100,000 cubic meters), and MDF boards (80,000 cubic meters) is expanding. A project for establishing glued laminated timber production on the basis of the Aursky sleeper impregnation plant with the capacity of more than 15,000 products annually may prove to be highly efficient.

The high efficiency of establishing added-value wood processing complexes is also worth mentioning. The construction of prefabricated wooden houses is scarcely developing in our country; however, it could solve many problems from the construction of cheap and easy reparable houses to the organization of cost efficient power and heat supply for small settlements scattered on wide and often remote territories of both the Far Eastern Federal District and other regions of the country. The social aspect is also very important in the context of using these regions' workforce.

## 4.4. SEAPORTS OF THE PACIFIC COAST REGION AND THE NORTHERN SEA ROUTE

### 4.4.1. SEAPORTS OF THE PACIFIC COAST REGION

Seaports on the Pacific Coast represent one of the key links between transportation and logistics infrastructures. They determine the accomplishment of the Far Eastern Federal District's competitive advantage, e.g., its geopolitical position that secures access to the World Ocean and countries of the Asia-Pacific Region. Thus, the development of ports is one of the most important conditions of the Far Eastern Federal District's socio-economic development.

Maritime transport satisfies the requirements of servicing mass import/export flows of raw materials and commodities in the region. Apart from light aviation, maritime transportation is the sole available mode of cargo carriages in the territories of Magadan, Sakhalin, and Kamchatka Oblast, as well as in the northern districts of Khabarovsk Krai. Along the Pacific coastline there are more than 20 commercial and 10 fishing seaports and about 300 harbors (according to the Register of the RF Seaports in the Pacific Coast basin)[42]. Notwithstanding the long period of freezing, year-round navigation is carried out in the following ports: Posyet, Zarubino, Vladivostok, Nakhodka, Magadan, Vanino, Vostochny, Petropavlovsk- Kamchatsky, Korsakov, and Kholmsk. There are about 200 navigational companies recorded in the Far Eastern Federal District and the following shipping companies perform activities there: FESCO (Far-Eastern), Sakhalin, Primorsky, Kamchatsky, Vostoktransflot, and Arkticheskaya.

The following ports have a potential circulation of no less than 1 million tons: Vostochny, Nakhodka, Vladivostok, and Posyet in Primorsky Krai; De-Kastri in Khabarovsk Krai; Kholmsk and Korsakov in Sakhalin; Magadan in Magadan Oblast; and Petropavlovsk-Kamchatsky in Kamchatka. The largest of these are identified in Table 4.3.

---

[42] http://www.morflot.ru/reestr_mp/

**TABLE 4.3.**   Largest Turnover of Pacific Coast Seaports in 2013[43]

| Seaport | 2013, in million tons | Growth by 2012, in percentages |
|---|---|---|
| Vostochny | 48.3 | 13.5% |
| Vanino | 23.8 | 16.8% |
| Vladivostok | 14.5 | 10.0% |
| Nakhodka | 18.4 | 8.1% |
| Prigorodnoe | 16.3 | −0.8% |
| De-Kastri | 7.0 | −4.9% |
| Pos'et | 5.6 | −3.0% |
| Total (Far East) | 144.8 | 7.8% |
| Including dry ports | 83.4 | 6.1% |
| Oil ports | 61.4 | 10.1% |

Ports that have direct access to the Trans-Siberian Railway and the Baikal-Amur Mainline and port railway stations together constitute transportation hubs. The large transportation hubs of the Far Eastern Federal District are located in Vladivostok (the commercial seaport of Vladivostok), Nakhodka (the commercial seaport of Nakhodka and the port of Vostochny), and in Vanino (the ports of Vanino and Sovetskaya Gavan). The largest general-purpose ports are as follows: Vostochny, Vanino, Vladivostok, and Nakhodka.

The main problems of ports in the Far Eastern Federal Districts are as follows:

- Insufficient capacity of a port caused by weak organization of carriages (long customs, border, and other administrative procedures);
- Lack of port-based communication lines and outdated equipment;
- Insufficient railway capacity (lack of carriage rolling stock, "narrowness" of border terminals, "abandoned" trains, etc.);
- The excessive specialization of Pacific Coast ports' capacities. By 2013, the cargo turnover of ports in the Far Eastern Federal District increased up to 145 million tons (Table 4.3); however, coal exported to markets in the Asia-Pacific region remains the main cargo.

Moreover, the main prospects of the port economy are also related to the operation of new coal terminals. Thus, at the end of 2013, an agreement

---

[43] http://www.rzd-partner.ru/

was signed for the construction of a specialized coal terminal in the area of Sukhodol Bay in Primorsky Krai with a capacity of 20 million tons annually. Construction on the coal terminal has already been started in Muchke Bay (the port of Vanino). Expected initial transshipment volumes are at the level of 15 million tons with prospective growth of up to 30 million tons.[44]

According to the information provided by the Association of Sea and Commercial Ports, the cargo turnover of seaports in Russia from January until November 2014 was 571.4 million tons. This ratio is 6% higher compared to the turnover for the same period of the previous year.[45]

The transshipment volume of bulk carriers amounted to 265.7 million tons (+13.7 %), which includes: 107.5 million tons of coal (+16.0%), 43,1, million tons of container cargo (+5.6%), 28,4 million tons of corn (+170%), 21.4 million tons of ferrous metals (+6.5%), 13.6 million tons of mineral fertilizers (+15.0%), 7.7 million tons of cargo on ferries (+30.2%), 4.4 million tons of timber cargos (+8.3%) and 4.2 million tons of scrap metals (+31.4 %). The volume of ore transshipment was reduced to 5.8 million tons (−15.0%) and non-ferrous metals decreased to 3.0 million tons (−14.1 %).

The volume of liquid cargo transshipment increased to 305.7 million tons (+0.2%), which includes: 173.8 million tons of crude oil (−8.7%), 117.4 million tons of petroleum products (+14.9%) and 11.1 million tons of liquid gas (+11.9%).

Seaports of the Pacific Coast basin increased the transshipment of cargo up to 149.7 million tons (+13.5 %), which includes up to 89.7 million tons of bulk carriers (+17.9%) and up to 60.0 million tons of liquid cargo (+7.4%). Cargo turnover was increased in the ports of Vostochny by up to 53.3 million tons (+20.8%), Vanino by up to 24.0 million tons (+11.0%), Nakhodka by up to 19.3 million tons (+15.9%), Prigorodnoye by up to 14.6 million tons (+0.3%), Vladivostok by up to 14.2 million tons (+6.5%), De Kastri by up to 7.3 million tons (+15.1 %) and Posyet by up to 6.2 million tons (+20.6%).[46]

The development of modern cargo carriages is distinguished by the growth of container cargo volumes. The end of 2013 showed that the

---

[44] http://www.riss.ru/analitika/2949-porty-dalnego-vostoka-osnova-uskorennogo-razvitiya-vostochnykh-territorij-strany#.VLkXv8kqFCA
[45,47] http://www.eg-online.ru/news/266859/

container turnover increased by 16% and thus comprised 1.56 million TEU. The majority of container carriages pass through the commercial seaport of Vladivostok (VMTP) (35%) and the port of Vostochny (30%). According to the VMTP development plan, the port capacity will increase from 500,000 to 650,000 TEU by 2015. It is expected that the capacity of the port of Vostochny will increase from 550,000 to 650,000 TEU.[47]

The further development of ports should include:

- Government support in the form of creating new economic zones and areas of advanced development;
- Improvement of organizational and administrative procedures for cargo handling;
- Emphasis on advanced development of container carriages;
- Development of unfrozen ports;
- Securing smooth carriages (in the context of port operations) on the Northern sea route.

## 4.4.2. THE NORTHERN SEA ROUTE

The project for joint development and exploration of the Northern Sea Route may become one of the offers that can entice foreign investors from European and North-Eastern Asian countries. Spreading from Cape Zhelaniya to Cape Dezhneva, the Northern Sea Route is targeted at the provision of sea carriers as the shorter and more economically advantageous transport corridor connecting Europe and Asia than the southern corridor (through the Suez Canal). The biggest part of it goes along Russian territory, practically from Murmansk to Petropavlovsk-Kamchatsky (the northern transport corridor). The usage of the Northern Sea Route through from Yokohama to Rotterdam leads to a shortcut by 35%, from 11,200 km to 7,300 km.[48]

The construction of a new deep-water port in Petropavlovsk-Kamchatsky can turn the administrative center of Kamchatka Krai into a large transportation hub for the acceptance and servicing of ships. The

---

[47] http://www.riss.ru/analitika/2949-porty-dalnego-vostoka-osnova-uskorennogo-razvitiya-vostoch-nykh-territorij-strany#.VLkXv8kqFCA
[48] East Russia Journal. Special Issue for the "Far East -2014" investment forum. September, 2014. Moscow-Petrapavlovsk-Kamchatsky.

Northern Sea Route is expected to be open for navigation for most of the year.

The development of the Northern Sea Route is essential for cargo transportation between Russian regions as well. The Northern Sea Route is almost twice as short as other sea routes from Europe to the Far East. The length of the main ice track of the Northern Sea Route from the Novozemelskiye straits to Port Provideniya is 5610 km; the length of navigational river routes adjacent to the Northern Sea Route is about 37000 km. Therefore, the Northern Sea Route is the most important part of the infrastructure of the Extreme North's economy and a connecting link between the Russian Pacific Coast region and western regions of the country. It comprises a single transportation network of the largest Siberian river waterways, and land, air, and pipeline transportation.

Foreign business circles' interest in the Northern Sea Route is determined by two key factors. First and utmost, it may become the most economically advantageous alternative to carriages that are made today between ports of Europe, the Far East, and North America. For instance, there are 6600 nautical miles in total from Hamburg to Yokohama on this route, while there are 11,400 miles through the Suez Canal. On the other hand, the Northern Sea Route appears to be interesting as a transport corridor for carriages of mineral raw materials from the arctic regions of Russia. 35% of the world oil and gas reserves are in the areas adjacent to it. Carriages of Russian gas and oil by sea may turn out to be even more advantageous than the construction and operation of gas and oil pipelines.

In addition, it is possible to arrange for carriage of mineral fertilizers from the Kola Peninsula to Eastern Asia and China on the Northern Sea Route. The promising volumes of carriages on the Northern Sea Route will correspond to the development of oil and gas deposits on the Yamal Peninsula, in the Ob and Yenisei River basins, as well as in the areas of the Barents Sea adjacent to the Northern Sea Route (the Timano-Pechorskaya petroleum province, the Shtokmanovskoye gas condensate, and the Prirazlomnoye oil deposit, etc.) and the development of oil and gas sea exportation from these deposits to Europe.

An incentive for the development of navigation in the eastern part of the Northern Sea Route may be the export of rare earth metals and apatites from the Tomtor arctic deposit in the Sakha (Yakutia) Republic and complex ores from the deposits in Chukotka to countries of the Asia-Pacific region. Commercial timber processing enterprises in the Yenisei and Lena River basins may develop with direct government support. There is a real possibility of increasing the volume of transit carriages on the Northern Sea Route by exporting ferrous metals and mineral fertilizers produced by exporting enterprises in the European part of Russia. The volumes of coastwise carriages on the Northern Sea Route will increase with the recovery of the arctic zone economy. According to a predictive estimate, the total volume of carriages on the Northern Sea Route will reach 14–15 million tons in 2015.

Also of note is an ambitious project for construction of a highway and a main railway line connecting the Far East with the Northern Sea Route through Chukotka. Significant reduction in length of carriages from Asia to Europe on such a route is evident. The creation of international concession for the realization of this project would lead to actual implementation.

## 4.5. ELECTRIC POWER INDUSTRY

The United Energy System of the Pacific Coast region takes in 3.1% of power consumption from the whole Russian power system (leaving out isolated energy areas of western and central Yakutia, Magadan Oblast, Chukotka, and Kamchatka Krai with Koryak Autonomous Okrug) that comprised 31.6 billion kWh in 2013 with an estimate of ~ 32 billion kWh in 2014.

In isolated energy areas of the Sakha (Yakutia) Republic, e.g., western and central areas, power consumption was 4.67 billion kWh or 72.5% of the total power consumption in the Sakha (Yakutia) Republic; these areas are expected to join the Eastern Integrated Power System within the period until 2020. The Yuzhno-Yakutsky energy area of the Sakha (Yakutia) Republic works within the Eastern Integrated Power System as well.

The implementation of major investment projects will trigger the growth of power demand. Significant volumes of electric power will be required by:

- Metallurgical productions and the creation of a mining and metallurgical cluster in the Amur River Region on the basis of ore deposits:

the Olekminsky mining and processing complex, the Garinsky mining and processing complex, and the Kimkano-Sutarsky mining and processing complex (in operation as of 2014);

- The creation of the Yuzhno-Yakutsky mining and metallurgical union on the basis of the Tayozhnoye and Desovskoye deposits (the mining and metallurgical company "Timir" Tayozhny mining and processing complex," which will be implemented in 2020);
- The extraction of coal in the territory of the Yuzhno-Yakutsky energy area, including development of the Elginsky coal deposit, construction of the Inaglinsky coal mining complex, and construction of the Chulmakanskaya mine;
- The development of gold ore deposits in Amur Oblast, including the Malomirsky, Pokrovsky, and Albinsky ore mines;
- Oil and gas refinery facilities corresponding to the development of main oil and gas pipeline systems; the largest project is the construction of the petrochemical complex "NK Rosneft" in Nakhodka (ZAO "VNHK" – the introduction of the first train is expected to take place in 2018);
- The project planned in Khabarovsky and Komsomolsky NPZ (oil refinery) in the territory of Amur Oblast (Berezovka settlement in the Ivanovsky district) to construct a complex for oil refinery and the transportation of petroleum products, called the "Amursky refinery," with a refinery capacity of up to 6 million tons of raw materials annually (with consideration for delivery of petroleum products to the domestic market and export to China);
- The development of shipbuilding enterprises on the basis of the Far Eastern Shipbuilding and Ship Repair Center, the principal directions of which are the modernization of ship-repairing facilities and the creation of new facilities for the implementation of projects to establish modern marine equipment and construct an offshore shipbuilding yard "Vostok-Raffls" (in Pyati Okhotnikov Bay) – Primorsky Krai;
- The implementation of the "Vostochny launch site" project in Amur Oblast (2014–2018);
- The development of seaports in Khabarovsk Krai (Sovetskaya Gavan, Vanino) and Primorsky Krai (Vladivostok, Posyet).

The general forecast of power consumption in the United Energy System of the Pacific Coast region within the period until 2020 is from 43.7 to 47.8 billion.

**TABLE 4.4.** Demand for Energy From the United Energy System of the Pacific Coast Region, MW (Basic Scenario)

| United Energy System of the Pacific Coast region | | | | | | | |
|---|---|---|---|---|---|---|---|
| | 2014 | 2015 | 2016 | 2017 | 2018 | 2019 | 2020 |
| Combined Maximum Load | 4644 | 4719 | 5583 | 5734 | 6165 | 6226 | 6273 |
| Statutory Reserve | 1069 | 1085 | 1284 | 1319 | 1418 | 1432 | 1443 |
| Export | 680 | 680 | 680 | 680 | 680 | 680 | 680 |
| Demand for Energy | 6393 | 6484 | 7547 | 7733 | 8263 | 8338 | 8396 |

**TABLE 4.5.** Demand for Energy From the United Energy System of the Pacific Coast Region, MW (Moderate-Optimistic Scenario)

| United Energy System of the Pacific Coast region at its Maximum Load | | | | | | | |
|---|---|---|---|---|---|---|---|
| | 2014 | 2015 | 2016 | 2017 | 2018 | 2019 | 2020 |
| Maximum Load | 5700 | 5891 | 7124 | 7419 | 7999 | 8117 | 8239 |
| Statutory Reserve | 1311 | 1355 | 1639 | 1706 | 1840 | 1867 | 1895 |
| Export | 680 | 680 | 680 | 680 | 680 | 680 | 680 |
| Demand for Energy | 7691 | 7926 | 9443 | 9805 | 10519 | 10664 | 10814 |

According to *INTER RAO UES*, the expected export delivery volume from the Eastern integrated power system to China in 2014 is 680 MW/3.3 billion kWh, and in the following period from 2015–2020, the expected volume is 680 MW/4.0 billion kWh.

The standard value of power reserve of the Eastern integrated power system makes up 23%.

The expected volumes of decommissioned generating capacities (leaving out the hydroelectric power stations of Rusgidro JSC within the Eastern integrated power system are as follows:

**TABLE 4.6.** The Expected Capacity of Decommissioned Energy Generating Facilities, MW

| | 2014 | 2015 | 2016 | 2017 | 2018 | 2019 | 2020 | Total from 2014 through 2020 |
|---|---|---|---|---|---|---|---|---|
| UESE*, total | 41.0 | | 144.0 | 35.0 | 217.5 | 65.0 | 48.0 | 550.5 |
| TPP** | 41.0 | | 144.0 | 35.0 | 217.5 | 65.0 | 48.0 | 550.5 |
| Including Central TPP | | | 7.0 | | 137.5 | | | 144.5 |
| CPP*** | 41.0 | | 137.0 | 35.0 | 80.0 | 65.0 | 48.0 | 406.0 |

* Starting from 2016, central and western power districts of the Sakha (Yakutia) Republic have been added to the United Energy System of the Pacific Coast region.
** TPP – Thermal Power Plant.
*** CPP – Condensing Power Plant.

Out of the total volume of planned introductions of generating capacities, the following generating objects have a high probability of implementation. These generating objects are included in the investment programs of Rushydro JSC, RAO UES Vostoka JSC, and DVEUK JSC.

**TABLE 4.7.** Additional Capacity of Power Generating Facilities with a High Probability of Implementation in the UESE, MW

| | 2014 | 2015 | 2016 | 2017 | 2018 | 2019 | 2020 | Total from 2014 through 2020 |
|---|---|---|---|---|---|---|---|---|
| UESE, total | 49.8 | 299.5 | 270.0 | | 845.0 | | | 1464.3 |
| Hydro Electric Power Plant | | 160.0 | 160.0 | | | | | 320.0 |
| TPP | 49.8 | 139.5 | 110.0 | | 845.0 | | | 1144.3 |
| Including central TPP | 49.8 | 139.5 | 110.0 | | 845.0 | | | 1144.3 |

**TABLE 4.8.**   The Capacity of Additional Power Generating Facilities Constructed by Company Owners, MW

| | 2014 | 2015 | 2016 | 2017 | 2018 | 2019 | 2020 | **Total from 2014 through 2020** |
|---|---|---|---|---|---|---|---|---|
| UESE, total | | | | 625.1 | 96.0 | 590.0 | 635.0 | 1946.1 |
| TPP | | | | 145.1 | | 590.0 | 635.0 | 1370.1 |
| Including central TPP | | | | 145.1 | | 590.0 | 635.0 | 1370.1 |
| REP | | | | 480.0 | 96.0 | | | 576.0 |
| Including Wind Farm | | | | 480.0 | 96.0 | | | 576.0 |

Table 4.9 provides information on the established capacity of power stations in the United Energy System of the Pacific Coast region. The correlation of the established capacity with the below data on the energy balance evidences availability of reserve capacities for the whole of the Far Eastern Federal District.

**TABLE 4.9.**   The Established Capacity of the United Energy System of the Pacific Coast Region, MW

| | **2013 Actual** | 2014 | 2015 | 2016 | 2017 | 2018 | 2019 | 2020 |
|---|---|---|---|---|---|---|---|---|
| UESE, total | 9061.0 | 9069.8 | 9369.3 | 11276.0 | 11337.0 | 11964.5 | 11899.5 | 11851.5 |
| Hydro Electric Power Plant | 3340.0 | 3340.0 | 3500.0 | 4617.5 | 4617.5 | 4617.5 | 4617.5 | 4617.5 |
| TPP | 5721.0 | 5729.8 | 5869.3 | 6658.5 | 6719.5 | 7347.0 | 7282.0 | 7234.0 |
| Including central TPP | 3712.5 | 3762.3 | 3901.8 | 4210.3 | 4210.3 | 4917.8 | 4917.8 | 4917.8 |
| CPP | 2005.0 | 1964.0 | 1964.0 | 2267.0 | 2328.0 | 2248.0 | 2183.0 | 2135.0 |
| Diesel | 3,5 | 3,5 | 3,5 | 181,2 | 181,2 | 181,2 | 181,2 | 181,2 |

Electric energy generation by hydroelectric power plants was taken into account in view of the long-term average annual ratio. The basic variant of the power generation estimate takes into account conditions of low water years for the United Energy System of the Pacific Coast region having a liberal share of hydroelectric power stations with generating capacities.

**TABLE 4.10.** The Energy Generating Structure of the United Energy System of the Russian Pacific Coast Region – Commissioned and Decommissioned Energy Generating Facilities (Including Modernized and Reconstructed Power Stations) with a High Probability of Implementation; the Basic Scenario

| Units of measure | Forecast | | | | | | | | | |
|---|---|---|---|---|---|---|---|---|---|---|
| | 2014 | | | | | 2020 | | | | |
| | NPP | HEPP | TPP | REP | Total | NPP | HEPP | TPP | REP | Total |
| Billion kW per hour | | 11.3 | 24.0 | 0.0 | 35.3 | | 16.7 | 31.0 | 0.0 | 47.7 |
| % | | 32.0 | 68.0 | 0.0 | 100.0 | | 34.9 | 65.1 | 0.0 | 100.0 |

**TABLE 4.11.** The Energy Generating Structure of the United Energy System of the Russian Pacific Coast Region – Commissioned and Decommissioned Energy Generating Facilities (Including Modernized and Reconstructed Power Stations) with a High Probability of Implementation; the Moderate-Optimistic Scenario

| Units of measure | Forecast | | | | | | | | | |
|---|---|---|---|---|---|---|---|---|---|---|
| | 2014 | | | | | 2020 | | | | |
| | NPP | HEPP | TPP | REP | Total | NPP | HEPP | TPP | REP | Total |
| Billion kW per hour | | 11.3 | 24.6 | 0.0 | 35.8 | | 16.7 | 35.1 | 0.0 | 51.8 |
| % | | 31.4 | 68.6 | 0.0 | 100.0 | | 32.2 | 67.8 | 0.0 | 100.0 |

The firm energy of hydroelectric power plants in the United Energy System of the Pacific Coast region under low water conditions will require supplemental fuel in order to cover the predicted level of power supply (million tons of coal equivalent).

**TABLE 4.12.** The Forecasted Level of Power Usage of the UESE (in Million Tons of Coal Equivalent)

| Forecast | | | | | | |
|------|------|------|------|------|------|------|
| **2014** | **2015** | **2016** | **2017** | **2018** | **2019** | **2020** |
| 1.1 | 1.2 | 1.2 | 1.4 | 1.5 | 1.5 | 1.5 |

**TABLE 4.13.** TPP's Need for Organic Fuel in the UESE for the Period From 2014 Through 2020; the Basic Scenario (in Million Tons of Coal Equivalent)

| Years | Total Usage | Gas | Oil | Coal | Other |
|------|------|------|------|------|------|
| 2014 | 11.214 | 3.353 | 0.259 | 7.603 | 0 |
| 2015 | 11.690 | 3.542 | 0.260 | 7.888 | 0 |
| 2016 | 12.519 | 4.225 | 0.274 | 8.020 | 0 |
| 2017 | 13.136 | 4.842 | 0.277 | 8.017 | 0 |
| 2018 | 13.451 | 5.144 | 0.278 | 8.028 | 0 |
| 2019 | 13.857 | 5.608 | 0.275 | 7.974 | 0 |
| 2020 | 13.958 | 5.690 | 0.273 | 7.995 | 0 |

**TABLE 4.14.** TPP's Need for Organic Fuel in the UESE for the Period from 2014 Through 2020; Moderate-Optimistic Scenario (in Million Tons of Coal Equivalent)

| Years | Total Usage | Gas | Oil | Coal | Other |
|------|------|------|------|------|------|
| 2014 | 11.428 | 3.422 | 0.259 | 7.746 | 0.00 |
| 2015 | 12.190 | 3.734 | 0.262 | 8.194 | 0.00 |
| 2016 | 13.432 | 4.503 | 0.276 | 8.653 | 0.00 |
| 2017 | 14.308 | 5.276 | 0.282 | 8.75 | 0.00 |
| 2018 | 14.797 | 5.678 | 0.283 | 8.836 | 0.00 |
| 2019 | 15.285 | 6.156 | 0.281 | 8.849 | 0.00 |

Within the period 2014–2020, construction is expected on the main power grid facilities securing power generation of the following major power stations: "VNHK" and Yakutskaya; and hydropower stations: Zagorskaya, Zelenchukskaya, Boguchanskaya, Nizhnebureiskaya.

The construction of new 500 kW power transmission lines in the Eastern integrated power system is based on the necessity of strengthening the main power system. That can be accomplished by an overhead transmission line of 500 kW Primorskaya – Khabarovksaya (the second

**TABLE 4.15.**  Electrical Balance in 2013, Million kW Per Hour

| | Electrical Energy Produced | Received from Abroad | Total Electrical Energy Consumed | Exported Abroad | Surplus (+)/ Deficit (−) of electrical energy |
|---|---|---|---|---|---|
| FEFD | 49806.7 | | 45505.0 | | 4301.7 |
| The Sakha (Yakutia) Republic | 8509.2 | 162.0 | 7182.6 | 1488.5 | 1326.6 |
| Kamchatka Krai | 1710.5 | 0.0 | 1710.5 | 0.0 | 0 |
| Primorsky Krai | 9451.0 | 3180.0 | 12631.0 | 0.0 | −3180 |
| Khabarovsk Krai | 8113.5 | 3609.0 | 8555.1 | 3167.4 | −441.6 |
| Amur Oblast | 15152.2 | 8636.0 | 7580.9 | 16207.3 | 7571.3 |
| Magadan Oblast | 2352.2 | 0.0 | 2205.5 | 146.7 | 146.7 |
| Sakhalin Oblast | 3952.9 | 0.0 | 3952.9 | 0.0 | 0 |
| Jewish Autonomous Oblast | 0.5 | 1143.7 | 1137.1 | 7.1 | −1136.6 |
| Chukotka Autonomous Okrug | 564.6 | 0.0 | 549.4 | 15.2 | 15.2 |

overhead transmission line), which is required for the considerable reduction of customer curtailments in Primorsky Krai under post emergency conditions by way of increasing the transit capacity between power systems in Khabarovsk Krai and Primorsky Krai.

Beginning in 2014, it is expected to combine the Siberian integrated power system and the Eastern integrated power system into networking by way of installing high voltage direct current links (hereinafter referred to as HVDC) with a capacity of ±200 MW on the 220 kW electric power substation Mogocha (the Siberian integrated power system) and on the 220 kW electric power substation Khani (2019) with the construction of a 220 kW overhead transmission line Tynda-Lopcha-Khani-Chara (the Eastern integrated power system) and transference to a 220 kW of 220 kW on the overhead transmission line Taksimo-Chara (the Siberian integrated power system).

The main trends in the 220 kW power systems development will consist in strengthening distribution functions and securing the power generation of power stations. 220 kW electric power lines of the power systems in the Pacific Coast region will qualify as the main electric power line.

During the period under review, it is planned to construct the main 220kW electrical grid facilities: construction of the 220 kW double-circuit overhead transmission line Tommot-Maya for combining the Yuzhny and Tsentralny energy areas of the Sakha (Yakutia) Republic; the 220 kW overhead transmission line Lensk – NPS-14 – NPS-15 – NPS-16 for external power supply of the oil pipeline system "VSTO" and for providing the possibility of combining the Zapadny and Yuzhny energy areas of the Sakha (Yakutia) Republic; construction of the 220 kW overhead transmission line Lensk-Peledui for the external power supply of the oil pipeline system "VSTO" and the possibility of connecting the Zapadny energy area of the Sakha (Yakutia) Republic on the UES of Russia.

In addition, for the purposes of securing the external power supply of the oil pipeline system "VSTO," it is planned to construct the following 220 kW electric power substations in the territory of the Sakha (Yakutia) Republic:

- The electric power substation NPS-19 in the Yuzhny energy area of the Sakha (Yakutia) Republic's power system;

- Three electric power substations NPS no. 10,11,15 in the Zapadny energy area of the Sakha (Yakutia) Republic's power system.

In addition, in accordance with the plans of "NK Rosneft," it is expected to construct an oil refinery ZAO "VNHK" with a customer contract demand of 372 MW and its own power station with the installed capacity of 632 MW in Primorsky Krai's power system; these are to be combined into networking with the Eastern integrated power system. For the purposes of securing the external power supply of the power receivers of ZAO "VNHK" and generation of power by TES ZAO "VNHK," it is planned to preliminarily construct two 220 kW overhead transmission lines from the 500 kW electric power substation Lozovaya to the applicant's electric power substation (the final volume will be determined based on the results of the development of an external power supply of power receivers and power generation by TES ZAO "VHNK").

Table 4.15 shows that, on the whole, the Far Eastern Federal District had excessive power consumption in 2013. The electric power surplus was concentrated in Amur Oblast, Yakutia, Magadan Oblast, and Chukotka.

## 4.6. CHEMICAL INDUSTRY

According to Rosstat's data for the year 2012, the chemical industry in the Far Eastern Federal District is represented only within article 13.44, "Plastic production at the stage of acquiring hydrocarbon monomers." The District's annual production volume is 2.1 thousand tons, which is approximately 0.04 % of the Russian average. This suggests that the chemical industry is not an industry specialization of the Far Eastern Federal District.

However, according to the current plans of some companies and public authorities of the Russian Federation's constituent entities that are part of the Far Eastern Federal District, this industry will be developed extensively in the following areas:

- Production of phosphate-magnesium fertilizer in the Sakha Republic;
- Production of nitrogen fertilizers, polypropene, polyethylene, gas-chemical and coal chemical products in Primorsky Krai;

- Production of mineral fertilizers and coal-chemical products in Amur Oblast;
- Production of coal-chemical products in Magadan Oblast;
- Production of oil- gas-chemical products in Sakhalin Oblast.

Export-oriented production will be developed within the abovementioned projects. In the long-term period, this will provide the industry with a competitive position that will accomplish national priorities in the Far Eastern Federal District.

# 4.7. MACHINE ENGINEERING AND METALLURGY

The main branches of machine engineering in Far Eastern Federal District are:

- the aircraft industry;
- shipbuilding;
- car manufacturing;
- the manufacture of agricultural equipment.

The percentages of machine engineering and metallurgy production in the volume of shipped products by the type of economic activity "processing industries" in the Far Eastern Federal District in 2012 were (in percentages based on actual prices):

- 26.4% of transport and equipment manufacturing (43.2% in Primorsky Krai, 27.4% in Khabarovsk Krai, and 19.1% in Amur Oblast);
- 6.4% of metallurgical production and production of finished metal products (22.9% in Magadan Oblast, 14.6% in Khabarovsk Krai, and 6.0% in Amur Oblast);
- 3.6% of cars and equipment manufacturing (15.5% in Magadan Oblast, 10.6% in the Sakha (Yakutia) Republic, and 9.2% in Sakhalin Oblast);
- 3.0% of electric equipment, and electronic and optical equipment (6.7% in the Republic of Sakha, 6.1% in Jewish Autonomous Oblast, and 4.5% in Primorsky Krai).

In general, machinery manufacturing in the Far Eastern Federal District is composed of assembly plants based on science-driven components imported to the region, including those from abroad. The cost of cars, equipment, and vehicles imported to the Far Eastern Federal District from abroad in 2012 was 5.3 billion US dollars, while the export from the region only achieved the figure of 690 million US dollars.

On average, the Far Eastern Federal District's economy possesses a similar level of investment attractiveness to the Russian economy in general (the return on assets is 5–9%). However, the relative investment attractiveness of the region abruptly drops in the productive industries, provided that the more producible an industry is, the lower the drop. The return on average assets in terms of the industries in the Far Eastern Federal District over the period of 2007–2012 made up 6% as compared to 11.6 % of the Russian average; 4.5% in processing industries as compared to 13.5%; 1% in machine engineering as compared to 6.2%; 4.1 % in the production of cars and equipment as compared to 8.5%; and 5.7% in the production of electric equipment, and electronic and optical equipment as compared to 10.6%.

The regional return on average assets made up 7.9% in the production of engines and turbines, except for aviation, auto, and motorcycle engines; 8.3% in the production of other lifting and handling equipment; and 5.7% in the production of machines used in crop farming.

Under such circumstances, the most attractive investment enterprises are the ones turning out products with a short payback period and using the least complicated production lines and processes. Generally, these are assembly plants as well as services for the maintenance of foreign equipment. This includes the production of equipment and machines for minerals extraction and construction, the production of cars, the production of appliances used for monitoring and controlling technical processes, and the production of optical equipment.

The largest such enterprises in the Far Eastern Federal District are those that produce vehicles and equipment. While the Russian average proportion of vehicles and equipment production in the context of the revenue of machine builders over the period of 2003–2012 was 42–48%, this ratio in the Far Eastern Federal District was 65–85%. More than a third of regional machine builders are engaged in the production and repair of vehicles and equipment (the biggest part of them is comprised of enterprises that repair and dispose of vessels). Approximately 70% of revenue, 66% of the Far Eastern workforce in machine engineering, 90% of assets, 90% of creditor indebtedness, and up to 100% of regional machine-building exports are concentrated in this field.

Objects of machine engineering in the Far Eastern Federal District ensuring Russia's global competitive advantages include:

- The rocket and space industry – the Far Eastern National Space Center on the basis of the "Vostochny launch site";
- The aircraft industry – the branch of the "Sukhoi Company" JSC "Komsomolsk-on-Amur Aircraft Production Association" named after Y.A. Gagarin.

A number of machine engineering industries in the Far Eastern Federal District ensure the achievement of the District's competitive advantages to the extent of the development of transportation and logistics systems, the extraction of minerals, and the promotion of the fishery complex; for example:

- Shipbuilding enterprises, including those affiliated with the Far Eastern Shipbuilding and Ship Repair Center (for example, "Dalnevostochny zavod "Zvezda," "Khabarovsky sudostroitelny zavod," "Amursky sudostroitelny zavod");
- The production of equipment for the handling of main oil and gas pipelines, geologic exploration, and the sinking and operation of wells (service companies, production of spare parts, measuring devices, etc.);
- The production of facilities for shelf development, including the construction of oil and gas platform units and oil tankers;
- The production of mining equipment ("Amursky Metallist");
- Service companies for maintaining the fishing industry and particularly for fish processing and servicing the fishing fleet in the coastal areas of the Far East.

The machine engineering and metal working industries of the Far Eastern Federal District should be fostered through various forms of public and private partnership. These include the creation of exclusive economic zones and areas of advanced development conforming to the main machine engineering trends of regions; particularly the shipbuilding and aviation industry in Primorky Krai and Khabarovsk Krai and machine engineering for the agricultural sector in Amur Oblast. The development of industries to some extent may also be promoted by the extension of state order for the recovery of a machine engineering production base.

**CHAPTER 5**

# DEFINING STRATEGIC COMPETITIVE ADVANTAGES OF THE RUSSIAN FEDERATION REGIONS ALLOCATED IN THE FAR EASTERN FEDERAL DISTRICT

In this section, the Russian Federation's strategic competitive advantages in the Far Eastern Federal District are presented based on regions and industries.

## 5.1. COMPETITIVE STRATEGIC ADVANTAGES OF THE RUSSIAN FEDERATION REGIONS IN THE FAR EASTERN FEDERAL DISTRICT

## 5.1.1. THE SAKHA (YAKUTIA) REPUBLIC

| Project | Interests | Projected Capacity | Date of Implementation | Project Cost | Competitive Advantages and Notes |
|---|---|---|---|---|---|
| **COAL INDUSTRY** | | | | | |
| Inalginsky mine, Chulmakansky and Denisovsk deposits | UK Kolmar (Gunvor and Volga Resources) | Up to 10.5 million tons | Until 2018 | 32.69 billion rubles | |
| Elga deposit | Mechel | 20.7 million tons | Until 2021 | 186.66 billion rubles | Open mining, capacity-more than 2 billion tons |
| **OIL AND GAS INDUSTRY** | | | | | |
| Chayanda field | Gazprom JSC | 61 billion cubic meters of gas | Until 2018 | | Connected to the Power of Siberia pipeline |
| Sredne-Tyunskoye field | Sakhatrans-neftegas JSC | More than 160 billion cubic meters | | | |
| Otradninskoye field | Sakhatrans-neftegas JSC | More than 100 billion cubic meters | | | |
| Kysyl – Syrskoye field | Yatec JSC (Summa group) | Around 400 billion cubic meters (unconfirmed) | | | |

## MINING INDUSTRY

| | | | | |
|---|---|---|---|---|
| **Gold** | | | | |
| Nezhdaninskoye deposit | Polyus Gold (Polyus group) | Around 680 tons | 16.5 billion rubles | |
| **Iron Ore** | | | | |
| Tayezhnoe deposit | EVRAZ group, ALROSA group | 4 million tons of concentrate per year | More than 10 billion rubles | 2300 job openings |
| Tarynmakhskoye and Gorgitskoye deposits | EVRAZ group, ALROSA group | 14.6 billion tons of concentrate per year | More than 56 billion rubles | |
| **Tin** | | | | |
| Deputatskoye deposit | Sakhaolove JSC | 198 thousand tons | | 13% of all Russian tin deposits. Company is bankrupt; mining has been halted. |
| **Lead, Zinc** | | | | |
| Verkhne-Menkechenskoye deposit | | 8 tons of lead, 8.5 thousand tons of zinc per year | More than 4 billion rubles | |

| Project | Interests | Projected Capacity | Date of Implementation | Project Cost | Competitive Advantages and Notes |
|---|---|---|---|---|---|
| Uranium Ore | | | | | |
| Elkon deposit | Rosatom | Around 600 thousands tons | | More than 90 billion rubles | The largest in the world. |
| Diamonds | | | | | |
| Aikhal, Myr, Udachnoe deposits. New deposit in Nyurbinsk Ulus | ALROSA group | Around 37 million carats | | | The largest producer in Russia. 168.5 billion rubles of revenue per year. |
| Rare Earth Metals | | | | | |
| Rare earth metals | Rostec | 42.7 million tons of conditioning ore | | | The largest in the world. Unique in composition and conditioning of rare earth metals. |
| **CHEMICAL INDUSTRY** | | | | | |
| Phosphorus and magnesium fertilizer production | ALROSA group | 3286 thousand tons of concentrate and 567 thousand tons of mineral fertilizer | | 47 billion rubles | The ROI period is 11.3 years. |

## 5.1.2. KAMCHATKA KRAI

| Project | Interests | Projected Capacity | Date of Implementation | Project Cost | Competitive Advantages and Notes |
|---------|-----------|--------------------|------------------------|--------------|----------------------------------|
| **DRINKING WATER** | | | | | |
| Extraction of natural drinking water in Russkaya Bay | Russkaya Voda JSC | 75 thousand cubic meters and up to 35 million bottles per year | | 1.4 billion rubles | The unique quality of the water containing silver. The ability to load vessels from the deposit. |
| **MINING INDUSTRY** | | | | | |
| Gold | | | | | |
| 11 gold mining objects | Zoloto Kamchatki | More than 440 tons | | More than 20 billion rubles | |
| **FISHING INDUSTRY** | | | | | |
| Construction and modernization of fish canning plant | Ozernovsky RKZ-55 JSC | 350 tons per day | | 1.2 billion rubles | One of the leaders of the fishing industry on the peninsular. |
| Modernization of the high-tech fish processing complex | Koryakmore product | 170 tons per day | | 500 million rubles | One of the largest fishing enterprises in the region. ROI is 3.5 years. |
| Creation of mariculture | Avacha-Tral | | | 745 million rubles | Occupies almost the entire sea urchin caviar market. |

## 5.1.3. PRIMORSKY KRAI

| Project | Interests | Projected Capacity | Date of Implementation | Project Cost | Competitive Advantages and Notes |
|---|---|---|---|---|---|
| **MINING INDUSTRY** | | | | | |
| Lead, Zinc | | | | | |
| Cheremshansky deposit, Maiminovsky deposit | GMK Dalpolimetall JSC | 26 million tons of lead, zinc and silver ore | | | Located near the existing mine complex. |
| **OIL AND GAS INDUSTRY** | | | | | |
| Liquefied natural gas production plant | Gazprom JSC | | 2014–2024 | 620–685 billion rubles | |
| **CHEMICAL INDUSTRY** | | | | | |
| Gas-and-chemical complex | ZAO National Chemical Group | | 1st stage: 2013–2017; 2nd stage: until 2020; 3rd stage: 1–4 years after the 2nd stage | 1st stage – 150 billion rubles | Nitrogen fertilizers production |
| Oil-and-chemical complex | Rosneft JSC | | 2013–2028 | 1496 billion rubles | Deep processing of oil and production of polypropylenes and polyethylenes. |

**TRANSPORTATION AND LOGISTICS INDUSTRY**

| Project | Company | Dates | Cost | Description |
|---|---|---|---|---|
| Sever universal handling complex | ZAO PO Primornefregasprom | 2016–2018 | 11 billion rubles | Construction of a modern coal shipment terminal (Vostochny) for export of coal. |
| The increase in turnover and the capacity of the Vostochny port | Vostochny port | 2013–2018 | 13.6 billion rubles | Ensuring coal export to the Asia-Pacific region. |
| Terminal Astafieva maritime bulk cargo terminal | Akva Resursy group | 1st stage: 2012–2014; 2nd stage: 2014–2019 | 4 billion rubles | Building additional facilities to increase export of coal to the Asia-Pacific countries. |
| Seaport construction | Kholdingovaya Kompaniya SDS-ugol JSC, LLC Sukhodol Seaport | 1st stage: 2014–2017; 2nd stage: 2017–2019; 3rd stage: 2019–2021 | 18 billion rubles | Ensuring coal export to Asia-Pacific region. |
| Vostochny – Nakhodka transport network | Rostransmodernizatsiya | 2012–2020 | 148 billion rubles | Developing the transport network: providing a full range of transport and logistics services for the processing of export and import, transit and coastal cargo containers. |

| Project | Interests | Projected Capacity | Date of Implementation | Project Cost | Competitive Advantages and Notes |
|---|---|---|---|---|---|
| Multimodal production and logistics complex | LLC Transit – DV Group | | 2013–2016 | 1.150 billion rubles | |
| Transportation and Logistics center of the "dry port" type | Akva Resursy group, LLC Magistral-DV | | 2013–2016 | 1.5 billion rubles | |
| Zarubino seaport | Summa group | | 2014–2020 | 60 billion rubles | Container terminal, bulk cargo terminal, grain terminal |
| **MECHANICAL ENGINEERING** Shipbuilding | | | | | |
| Zvezda shipbuilding complex | United Shipbuilding Corporation JSC | LNG – 4 units; Tankers – 5 units; floating modules – 1 units. | 2010–2018 | 111.7 billion rubles | Tankers of up to 350 thousand tons, LNG, ice-class vessels, specialized vessels, elements of marine platforms and other marine equipment production. |

## 5.1.4. KHABAROVSK KRAI

| Project | Interests | Projected Capacity | Date of Implementation | Project Cost | Competitive Advantages and Notes |
|---|---|---|---|---|---|
| **MINING INDUSTRY** | | | | | |
| Platinum | | | | | |
| Konder, Galmoenan, Uorlagan deposits | Russkaya Platina group | More than 15 tons available | | | 2000 job openings |
| Tin | | | | | |
| Pravourmiyskoye deposit | Russkoye olovo JSC | 3000 tons of concentrated tin | Until 2017 | 8.2 billion rubles | |
| **OIL AND GAS INDUSTRY** | | | | | |
| Oil and Gas refinery complex | LLC RN-Komsomolsky NPZ | | | | Deep oil refinery (aviation and motor gasoline, jet fuel, diesel fuel). |
| **MECHANICAL ENGINEERING** | | | | | |
| Power Plant Engineering | | | | | |
| Construction of a gas turbine plant in Khabarovsk | Direktsiya stroyushegosya Khabarovskogo gazoturbinnogo zavoda JSC | | Until 2018 | 51 billion rubles | |

**TRANSPORTATION AND LOGISTICS INDUSTRY**

| | | | | |
|---|---|---|---|---|
| Transportation and logistics center at the Khabarovsk Novy Airport | Khabarovsk Aeroport JSC, Incheon International Airport Corporation and Daewoo Engineering Company (South Korea) | 2014–2018 | 18.8 billion rubles | |

**FOREST INDUSTRY**

| | | | | |
|---|---|---|---|---|
| Far Eastern center of deep wood processing | RFP Group Holding | Until 2019 | 12.1 billion rubles | |

**FISHING INDUSTRY**

| | | | | |
|---|---|---|---|---|
| Fishing industry complex | | | 13.8 billion rubles | Sovetskaya Gavan special port economic zone, Lososin settlement |

## 5.1.5. AMUR OBLAST

| Project | Interests | Projected Capacity | Date of Implementation | Project Cost | Competitive Advantages and Notes |
|---|---|---|---|---|---|
| **MINING INDUSTRY** | | | | | |
| Iron Ore | | | | | |
| Olekminsk Mine | Petropavlovsk company group | 1.2 million tons of concentrate | | More than 19 billion rubles | Creation of the unique iron ore cluster on the basis of Kimkan – Sutar and Garinsky deposits. |
| Garinsky Mine | Up to 10 million tons of concentrate | | Up to 2016 | | |
| Polymetals | | | | | |
| Kun-Manyo Copper-nickel deposit | Amur Minerals Corp. | More than 200 thousand tons of nickel; more than 55 thousand tons of copper | | 34 billion rubles | |

## 5.1.6. MAGADAN OBLAST

| Project | Interests | Projected Capacity | Date of Implementation | Project Cost | Competitive Advantages and Notes |
|---|---|---|---|---|---|
| **COAL INDUSTRY** | | | | | |
| Yuzhno-Omolonsk deposit | | More than 440 million tons available | | | |
| **MINING INDUSTRY** | | | | | |
| Gold | | | | | |
| Natalkinskoye deposit | Polyus-Zoloto JSC (Polyus Group) | 1449 tons available | | | The largest deposit in Russia. |
| Yuzhno-Omolonsk deposit | Polymetal International PLC | 650 tons available | | | |
| Polymetals | | | | | |
| Yuzhno-Omolonsk deposit | | 4 million tons of copper (est.), 400 thousand tons of Molybdenum | | | The largest deposit in Russia. |

| Project | Interests | Projected Capacity | Date of Implementation | Project Cost | Competitive Advantages and Notes |
|---|---|---|---|---|---|
| Iron Ore | | | | | |
| Yuzhno–Omolonsk deposit | | 760 million tons (est) | | | |
| FISHING INDUSTRY | | | | | |
| Creation of fishery cluster | | | | 500 million rubles | As part of the project: reconstruct Magadan fishing port, reconstruct and construct salmon fish factories. |

## 5.1.7. SAKHALIN OBLAST

| Project | Interests | Projected Capacity | Date of Implementation | Project Cost | Competitive Advantages and Notes |
|---|---|---|---|---|---|
| **COAL INDUSTRY** | | | | | |
| Soltsevsky coal deposit | LLC Sakhalin Ugol-2 (Eastern Mining Company) | 1.2 million tons per year | Until 2017 | 2.4 billion rubles | |
| **OIL AND GAS INDUSTRY** | | | | | |
| Sakhalin-1 Project | Rosneft | 307 million tons of oil and 485 billion cubic meters of gas (est.) | | | |
| Sakhalin-2 Project | Gazprom JSC | 174 million tons of oil and 635 billion cubic meters of gas | 2014–2019 | | |
| Sakhalin-3 Project | Rosneft and Gazprom JSC | 700 million tons of oil and 1.3 trillion cubic meters of gas | Until 2025 | 1200 million rubles | |

**CHEMICAL INDUSTRY**

| | | | | |
|---|---|---|---|---|
| Oil and Gas Chemical production | | 2013–2025 | 158.5 billion rubles | |

**FISHING INDUSTRY**

| | | | | |
|---|---|---|---|---|
| The construction of 9 salmon farms | ZAO Gydrostory | 2014–2016 | 2 billion rubles | |
| Marine biotechnological park | 30 thousand tons per year | Until 2035 | 1.6 billion rubles | Commercial cultivation and deep processing of aquatic species (sea cucumber, scallop). |

## 5.1.8. JEWISH AUTONOMOUS OBLAST

| Project | Interests | Projected Capacity | Date of Implementation | Project Cost | Competitive Advantages and Notes |
|---|---|---|---|---|---|
| **MINING INDUSTRY** | | | | | |
| Iron Ore | | | | | |
| Kimkano-Sutarsky mine | Petrapavlovsk group | 4.5 million tons of graphite concentrate per year | 2015 | Around 24 billion rubles | Forms a cluster together with Olekminsk and Garinsk mines. |
| Graphite | | | | | |
| Soyuznoe deposit development | LLC Dalnevostochny Grafit, Magnezit group | 40 thousand tons of graphite concentrate | Until 2018 | Around 4 billion rubles | The largest deposit in Russia |
| **TRANSPORTATION AND LOGISTICS INDUSTRY** | | | | | |
| Construction of the railway bridge across the Amur River on the Russian-Chinese state border in the Nizhneleninskoye settlement | Development of the Far East Fund and Direct Investment Fund | | 2016 | Around 8 billion rubles | |

## 5.1.9. CHUKOTKA AUTONOMOUS OKRUG

| Project | Interests | Projected Capacity | Date of Implementation | Project Cost | Competitive Advantages and Notes |
|---|---|---|---|---|---|
| **COAL INDUSTRY** | | | | | |
| Bering coal deposit | Tigers Realm Coal LTD | More than 4 billion tons available | Until 2021 | 130 billion rubles | |
| **MINING INDUSTRY** | | | | | |
| Polymetals | | | | | |
| Chaun-Bilibinsky production zone | | More than 500 thousand tons of tin, 24 million tons of copper | | 94.8 billion rubles | |
| **REINDEER HERDING, SEA MAMMAL HUNTING** | | | | | |
| Organization of processing of reindeer and sea hunting products (antlers, skin, tallow) | | | | For the reindeer – 353 million rubles; for the sea mammal hunting – 57 million rubles | |

## 5.2. INDUSTRY-SPECIFIC STRATEGIC COMPETITIVE ADVANTAGES IN THE FAR EASTERN FEDERAL DISTRICT

| Project | Interests | Projected Capacity | Date of Implementation | Project Cost | Competitive Advantages and Notes | Region |
|---|---|---|---|---|---|---|
| **COAL INDUSTRY** | | | | | | |
| Inaglinsky mine, Chulmakansky and Denisovsky deposit | UK Kolmar (Gunvor and Volga Resources) | Up to 10.5 million tons | Through 2018 | 32.69 billion rubles | | The Sakha (Yakutia) Republic |
| Elga deposit | Mechel | 20.7 million tons | Through 2021 | 186.66 billion rubles | Open mining, capacity -more than 2 billion tons | The Sakha (Yakutia) Republic |
| Yuzhno-Omolonsk deposit | | More than 440 million tons available | | | | Magadan Oblast |
| Soltsevsky coal deposit | LLC Sakhalin Ugol-2 (Eastern Mining Company) | 1.2 million tons per year | Through 2017 | 2.4 billion rubles | | Sakhalin Oblast |
| Bering coal deposit | Tigers Realm Coal LTD | More than 4 billion tons available | Through 2021 | 130 billion rubles | | Chukotka Autonomous Okrug |

## OIL AND GAS INDUSTRY

| | | | | | | |
|---|---|---|---|---|---|---|
| Chayanda field | Gazprom JSC | 61 billion cubic meters of gas | Through 2018 | | Connected to the Power of Siberia pipeline | The Sakha (Yakutia) Republic |
| Sredne-Tyunskoye field | Sakhatrans-neftegas JSC | More than 160 billion cubic meters | | | | The Sakha (Yakutia) Republic |
| Otradninskoye field | Sakhatrans-neftegas JSC | More than 100 billion cubic meters | | | | The Sakha (Yakutia) Republic |
| Kysyl – Syrskoye field | Yatec JSC (Summa group) | Around 400 billion cubic meters (unconfirmed) | | | | The Sakha (Yakutia) Republic |
| Liquefied natural gas production plant | Gazprom JSC | | 2014–2024 | 620–685 billion rubles | | Primorsky Krai |
| Oil and Gas refinery complex | LLC RN-Komsomolsky NPZ | | | | Deep oil refinery (aviation and motor gasoline, jet fuel, diesel fuel) | Khabarovsk Krai |
| Sakhalin-1 Project | Rosneft | 307 million tons of oil and 485 billion cubic meters of gas (est.) | | | | Sakhalin Oblast |
| Sakhalin-2 Project | Gazprom JSC | 174 million tons of oil and 635 billion cubic meters of gas | 2014–2019 | | | Sakhalin Oblast |

| Project | Interests | Projected Capacity | Date of Implementation | Project Cost | Competitive Advantages and Notes | Region |
|---|---|---|---|---|---|---|
| Sakhalin-3 Project | Rosneft and Gazprom JSC | 700 million tons of oil and 1.3 trillion cubic meters of gas | Through 2025 | 1200 million rubles | | Sakhalin Oblast |
| MINING INDUSTRY | | | | | | |
| Gold | | | | | | |
| Nezhdaninskoye deposit | Polyus Gold (Polyus group) | Around 680 tons | | 16.5 billion rubles | | The Sakha (Yakutia) Republic |
| 11 gold mining objects | Zoloto Kamchatki | More than 440 tons | | More than 20 billion rubles | | Kamchatka Krai |
| Natalkinskoye deposit | Polyus-Zoloto JSC (Polyus Group) | 1449 tons available | | | The largest deposit in Russia | Magadan Oblast |
| Yuzhno-Omolonsk deposit | Polymetal International PLC | 650 tons available | | | | Magadan Oblast |
| Iron Ore | | | | | | |
| Tayezhnoe deposit | EVRAZ group, ALROSA group | 4 million tons of concentrate per year | | More than 10 billion rubles | 2300 job openings | The Sakha (Yakutia) Republic |
| Tarynnakhskoye and Gorgitskoye deposits | EVRAZ group, ALROSA group | 14.6 billion tons of concentrate per year | | More than 56 billion rubles | | The Sakha (Yakutia) Republic |

| Project | Interests | Projected Capacity | Date of Implementation | Project Cost | Competitive Advantages and Notes | Region |
|---|---|---|---|---|---|---|
| Olekminsk Mine | Petropavlovsk group | 1.2 million tons of concentrate | Through 2016 | More than 19 billion rubles | Creation of the unique iron ore cluster on the basis of Kimkan – Sutar and Garinsky deposits | Amur Oblast |
| Garinsky Mine | | Up to 10 million tons of concentrate | | | | Amur Oblast |
| Yuzhno-Omolonsk deposit | | 760 million tons (est) | | | | Magadan Oblast |
| Kimkano-Sutarsky mine | Petrapavlovsk group | 4.5 million tons of graphite concentrate per year | 2015 | Around 24 billion rubles | Forms a cluster together with Olekminsk and Garinsk mines | Jewish Autonomous Oblast |
| Tin | | | | | | |
| Deputatskoye deposit | Sakhaolove JSC | 198 thousand tons | | | 13% of all Russian tin deposits. Company is bankrupt; mining has been halted. | The Sakha (Yakutia) Republic |
| Pravourmiyskoye deposit | Russkoye olovo JSC | 3000 tons of concentrated tin | Through 2017 | 8.2 billion rubles | | Khabarovsk Krai |

| Project | Interests | Projected Capacity | Date of Implementation | Project Cost | Competitive Advantages and Notes | Region |
|---|---|---|---|---|---|---|
| **Lead, Zinc** | | | | | | |
| Verkhne-Menkechenskoye deposit | | | 8 tons of lead, 8.5 thousand tons of zinc per year | More than 4 billion rubles | | The Sakha (Yakutia) Republic |
| Cheremshansky deposit, Maiminovsky deposit | GMK Dalpolimetall JSC | | 26 million tons of lead, zinc and silver ore | | Located near the existing mine complex. | Primorsky Krai |
| **Uranium Ore** | | | | | | |
| Elkon deposit | Rosatom | Around 600 thousands tons | | More than 90 billion rubles | The largest in the world. | The Sakha (Yakutia) Republic |
| **Diamonds** | | | | | | |
| Aikhal, Myr, Udachnoe deposits. New deposit in Nyurbinsk Ulus | ALROSA group | Around 37 million carats | | | The largest producer in Russia. 168.5 billion rubles of revenue per year. | The Sakha (Yakutia) Republic |
| **Rare Earth Metals** | | | | | | |
| Rare earth metals | Rostec | | 42.7 million tons of conditioning ore | | The largest in the world. Unique in composition and conditioning of rare earth metals. | The Sakha (Yakutia) Republic |

| Project | Interests | Projected Capacity | Date of Implementation | Project Cost | Competitive Advantages and Notes | Region |
|---|---|---|---|---|---|---|
| **Platinum** | | | | | | |
| Konder, Galmoenan, Uorlagan deposits | Russkaya Platina group | More than 15 tons available | | | 2000 job openings | Khabarovsk Krai |
| **Polymetals** | | | | | | |
| Kun-Manyo Copper-nickel deposit | Amur Minerals Corp. | More than 200 thousand tons of nickel; more than 55 thousand tons | | 34 billion rubles | | Amur Oblast |
| Yuzhno-Omolonsk deposit | | 4 million tons of copper (est.), 400 thousand tons of Molybdenum | | | The largest deposit in Russia | Magadan Oblast |
| Chaun-Bilibinsky production zone | | More than 500 thousand tons of tin, 24 million tons of copper | | 94.8 billion rubles | | Chukotka Autonomous Okrug |
| **Graphite** | | | | | | |
| Soyuznoe deposit development | LLC Dalnevostochny Grafit, Magnezit group | 40 thousand tons of graphite concentrate | Through 2018 | Around 4 billion rubles | The largest deposit in Russia. | Jewish Autonomous Oblast |

## CHEMICAL INDUSTRY

| Project | Interests | Projected Capacity | Date of Implementation | Project Cost | Competitive Advantages and Notes | Region |
|---|---|---|---|---|---|---|
| Phosphorus and magnesium fertilizer production | ALROSA group | 3286 thousand tons of concentrate and 567 thousand tons of mineral fertilizer | | 47 billion rubles | The ROI period is 11.3 years. | The Sakha (Yakutia) Republic |
| Gas-and-chemical complex | ZAO National Chemical Group | | 1st stage: 2013–2017; 2nd stage: Through 2020; 3rd stage: 1–4 years after the 2nd stage | 1st stage – 150 billion rubles | Nitrogen fertilizers production. | Primorsky Krai |
| Oil-and-chemical complex | Rosneft JSC | | 2013–2028 | 1496 billion rubles | Deep processing of oil and production of polypropylenes and polyethylenes | Primorsky Krai |
| Oil and Gas Chemical production | | | 2013–2025 | 158.5 billion rubles | | Sakhalin Oblast |

| Project | Interests | Projected Capacity | Date of Implementation | Project Cost | Competitive Advantages and Notes | Region |
|---|---|---|---|---|---|---|
| **DRINKING WATER** | | | | | | |
| Extraction of natural drinking water in Russkaya Bay | Russkaya Voda JSC | 75 thousand cubic meters and up to 35 million bottles per year | | 1.4 billion rubles | The unique quality of the water containing silver. The ability to load vessels from the deposit | Kamchatka Krai |
| **FISHING INDUSTRY** | | | | | | |
| Construction and modernization of fish canning plant | Ozernovsky RKZ-55 JSC | 350 tons per day | | 1.2 billion rubles | One of the leaders of the fishing industry on the peninsular | Kamchatka Krai |
| Modernization of the high-tech fish processing complex | Koryakmoreproduct | 170 tons per day | | 500 million rubles | One of the largest fishing enterprises in the region. ROI is 3.5 years | Kamchatka Krai |
| Creation of mariculture | Avacha-Tral | | | 745 million rubles | Occupies almost the entire sea urchin caviar market | Kamchatka Krai |
| Fishing industry complex | | | | 13.8 billion rubles | Sovetskaya Gavan special port economic zone, Lososin settlement | Khabarovsk Krai |

| Project | Interests | Projected Capacity | Date of Implementation | Project Cost | Competitive Advantages and Notes | Region |
| --- | --- | --- | --- | --- | --- | --- |
| Creation of fishery cluster | | | | 500 million rubles | As part of the project: reconstruction of Magadan fishing port, reconstruction and construction of salmon fish factories. | Magadan Oblast |
| The construction of 9 salmon farms | ZAO Gydrostory | | 2014–2016 | 2 billion rubles | | Sakhalin Oblast |
| Marine biotechnological park | | 30 thousand tons per year | Through 2035 | 1.6 billion rubles | Commercial cultivation and deep processing of aquatic species (sea cucumber, scallop). | Sakhalin Oblast |
| **TRANSPORTATION AND LOGISTICS INDUSTRY** | | | | | | |
| Sever universal handling complex | ZAO PO Primorneftegasprom | | 2016–2018 | 11 billion rubles | Construction of a modern coal shipment terminal (Vostochny) for export of coal. | Primorsky Krai |

| Project | Interests | Projected Capacity | Date of Implementation | Project Cost | Competitive Advantages and Notes | Region |
|---|---|---|---|---|---|---|
| The increase in turnover and the capacity of the Vostochny port | | Vostochny port | 2013–2018 | 13.6 billion rubles | Ensuring coal export to Asia-Pacific region. | Primorsky Krai |
| Terminal Astafieva maritime bulk cargo terminal | | Akva Resursy group | 1st stage: 2012–2014; 2nd stage: 2014–2019 | 4 billion rubles | Building additional facilities to increase export of coal to the Asia-Pacific countries. | Primorsky Krai |
| Seaport construction | | Kholdingovaya Kompaniya SDS-ugol JSC, LLC Sukhodol Seaport | 1st stage: 2014–2017; 2nd stage: 2017–2019; 3rd stage: 2019–2021 | 18 billion rubles | Ensuring coal export to Asia-Pacific region. | Primorsky Krai |
| Vostochny – Nakhodka transport network | | Rostransmodernizatsiya | 2012–2020 | 148 billion rubles | Development of the transport network: providing a full range of transport and logistics services for the processing of export and import, transit and coastal cargo containers. | Primorsky Krai |

| Project | Interests Projected Capacity | Date of Implementation | Project Cost | Competitive Advantages and Notes | Region |
|---|---|---|---|---|---|
| Multimodal production and logistics complex | LLC Transit – DV Group | 2013–2016 | 1.150 billion rubles | | Primorsky Krai |
| Transportation and Logistics center of the "dry port" type | Akva Resursy group, LLC Magistral-DV | 2013–2016 | 1.5 billion rubles | | Primorsky Krai |
| Zarubino seaport | Summa group | 2014–2020 | 60 billion rubles | Container terminal, bulk cargo terminal, grain terminal | Primorsky Krai |
| Transportation and logistics center at the Khabarovsk Novy Airport | Khabarovsk Aeroport JSC, Incheon International Airport Corporation and Daewoo Engineering Company (South Korea) | 2014–2018 | 18.8 billion rubles | | Khabarovsk Krai |
| Construction of the railway bridge across the Amur River on the Russian-Chinese state border in the Nizhneleninsk-oye settlement | Development of the Far East Fund and Direct Investment Fund | 2016 | Around 8 billion rubles | | Jewish Autonomous Oblast |

| Project | Interests | Projected Capacity | Date of Implementation | Project Cost | Competitive Advantages and Notes | Region |
|---|---|---|---|---|---|---|
| **MECHANICAL ENGINEERING** | | | | | | |
| Shipbuilding | | | | | | |
| Zvezda shipbuilding complex | United Shipbuilding Corporation JSC | LNG – 4 units; Tankers – 5 units; floating modules – 1 units. | 2010–2018 | 111.7 billion rubles | Tankers of up to 350 thousand tons, LNG, ice-class vessels, specialized vessels, elements of marine platforms and other marine equipment production. | Primorsky Krai |
| Power Plant Engineering | | | | | | |
| Construction of a gas turbine plant in Khabarovsk | Direktsiya stroyushegosya Khabarovskogo gazoturbinnogo zavoda JSC | | Through 2018 | 51 billion rubles | | Khabarovsk Krai |
| **FOREST INDUSTRY** | | | | | | |
| Far Eastern center of deep wood processing | RFP Group Holding | | Through 2019 | 12.1 billion rubles | | Khabarovsk Krai |

| Project | Interests | Projected Capacity | Date of Implementation | Project Cost | Competitive Advantages and Notes | Region |
|---|---|---|---|---|---|---|
| **REINDEER HERDING, SEA MAMMAL HUNTING** | | | | | | |
| Organization of processing of reindeer and sea hunting products (antlers, skin, tallow) | | | | For the reindeer – 353 million rubles; for the sea mammal hunting – 57 million rubles | | Chukotka Autonomous Okrug |

## 5.3. STRATEGIC OBSERVATIONS

Competitive advantages of the Far Eastern Federal District are located in the following industries by regions:

### The Sakha (Yakutia) Republic:
- Coal industry;
- Mining industry (gold, iron ore, tin, polymetals, uranium ore, diamonds, rare earth metals);
- Oil and gas industry;
- Chemical industry.

### Kamchatka Krai:
- Drinking water;
- Mining industry (gold);
- Fishing industry.

### Primorsky Krai:
- Mining industry;
- Oil and gas industry;
- Chemical industry;
- Mechanical engineering (shipbuilding);
- Transportation and logistics industry.

### Khabarovsk Krai:
- Mining industry (platinum, tin);
- Oil and gas industry;
- Mechanical engineering (power plant engineering);
- Transportation and logistics industry;
- Forest industry;
- Fishing industry.

### Amur Oblast:
- Mining industry (iron ore, polymetals).

### Magadan Oblast:

- Coal industry;
- Mining industry (gold, iron ore, polymetals);
- Fishing industry.

### Sakhalin Oblast:

- Coal industry;
- Oil and gas industry;
- Chemical industry;
- Fishing industry.

### Jewish Autonomous Oblast:

- Mining industry (iron ore, graphite);
- Transportation and logistics industry.

### Chukotka Autonomous Okrug:

- Coal industry;
- Mining industry (polymetals);
- Reindeer herding, sea mammal hunting.

It should be noted that the development of the Northern Sea Route enables Russia's competitive advantage in the transportation and logistics cluster.

This summary might be used for the formulation of the problem and its solution on the basis of economic and mathematical modeling of priority development projects.

# CHAPTER 6

# STRATEGIC PROSPECTS FOR THE DEVELOPMENT OF PUBLIC–PRIVATE PARTNERSHIP

## 6.1. PUBLIC–PRIVATE PARTNERSHIP: THE GLOBAL PRACTICE

The political, economic and social changes of the last two decades in countries with a transition economy, as well as the intensive process of globalization, have become the grounds for bringing together government and business communities. For the majority of countries, the past few years have been a struggle to achieve an effective strategy for economic development with the help of competitive advantages through the development of key elements of national infrastructure. This has led the state to increased interest in private companies, particularly in the use of their capacity to finance, build, and implement special projects aimed at developing the country's infrastructure. Thus, the public–private partnership (PPP) is developing rapidly and is of great interest throughout the world. The scope of public–private partnerships in foreign countries is very diverse and represents a wide range of business models and relationships. Within these partnerships, resources drawn from the private sector can vary: from funds to know-how and managerial practice.

The term "public–private partnership" refers to diverse schemes of project implementation that, unlike privatization or "joint ventures," are already well known in our country. Abroad, it is more common to use the English abbreviation "PPP" from the phrase "public private partnership."

Increasingly, public–private partnership is viewed as one of the most effective mechanisms to meet the shortfalls of funds for infrastructure development in the majority of countries. Foreign countries have made significant progress in advancing public–private partnership. In this regard, the usage of long-term methodology and the practice of PPP instruments by foreign countries is appropriate. Without studying the successful achievements of the most developed countries in the world, this approach cannot be implemented in our country immediately.

Leaders in the field of public–private partnerships are the United States, Britain, France, and Germany. According to the National Council for Public–Private Partnerships (National Council for Public–Private Partnership), in the United States of the 65 basic types of activities that the municipal authorities perform (water works, sewage works, garbage collection, schooling, parking lots managing, etc.), a normal city uses commercial firms in 23 cases.

During the first half of 2014, the total project financing of PPP by country was as follows:

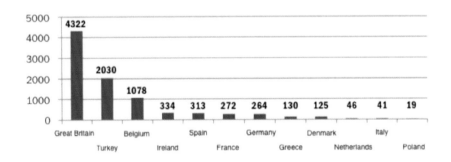

**FIGURE 6.1.**   The Total Project Financing for PPP During the First Half of 2014 in European Countries (Millions of Euros).[49]

Meanwhile, the total number of projects implemented in these countries was as follows:

<hr />

[49] Composed on the basis of information from European PPP Expertise Centre. http://www.eib.org/epec/

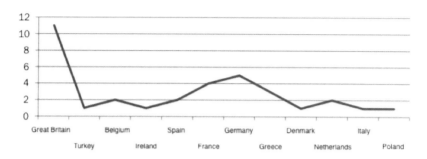

**FIGURE 6.2.**   The Number of Projects Implemented in the First Half of 2014 in European Countries on the Basis of PPP.[50]

The following are examples of PPP projects, implemented by EU authorities:

- In France – construction of the "Brittany – Loire" railroad and Disneyland;
- In Portugal – "Vasco da Gama" bridge, and the Redo and Tara power stations;
- In Greece – Spata (Athens) Airport, and the Corinth Canal Bridge.

PPP in foreign countries as a form of interaction between the state and private business is not new. The start of PPP began in the transport industry. The first roads that interconnected US cities were built by private companies and were toll roads. In 1792, the state of Pennsylvania registered the first private company to construct a road from Philadelphia to Lancaster. In the period from 1792 to 1845, 11 of the 13 original states had registered more than fifteen hundred road companies, although about one-third of them had not built a single mile of road. The profitability of road projects was not very high, but the shares were successfully placed among the population; people viewed their contributions not only as the allocation of capital, but also as the development of their areas. During the construction of the first transcontinental railroads in the United States, federal lands, adjacent to the roadbed, were often transferred to railway companies. The increasing value of these lands after the completion of the project greatly increased the attractiveness of railway construction to private investors.

---

[50] See footnote 4.

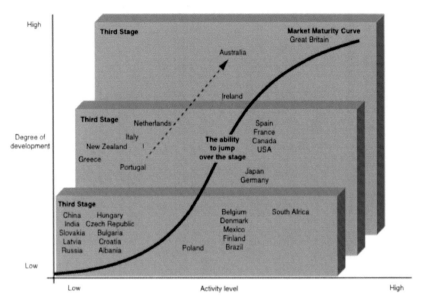

**FIGURE 6.3.** The PPP market maturity curve.[51]

Presently, PPP road construction projects include financing new toll roads, constructing, and investing in the replacement of old tollbooths for a modern remote system that does not require cars to reduce their speed while passing through them. Increasing discussions are being held over whether to transfer certain lanes on toll-free roads to private management to organize fast toll roads.[52]

Figure 6.3 clearly shows how countries are moving up the "maturity curve" and resisting the desire to implement PPP projects in those areas where necessary conditions do not yet exist. Despite the fact that PPP projects make a profit, they also face great challenges. There is a danger that the hasty transfer of assets to a private partner without careful examination by the public sector can lead to the risk of losing vital services for the population as a whole. Thus, an important task for PPP is the development of institutions, procedures, and processes for their effective organization.

[51] A separate segment for private investment is the maintenance of order on the roads. The private sector can take on responsibilities such as call handling and accident reports, and monitoring the situation on the roads. Insurance companies interested in investigating accidents can successfully reduce costs to the state road police.

[52] Source: Deloitte and Touche USA LLP.

This problem can be defined as a strengthening of management potential. While moving up the curve, the authorities should pay due attention to the management system's improvement.

The analysis of foreign experience with PPP has shown that each country has its own priority sectors for the use of PPP. There exists a correlation between the level of development of the country and the industry that is selected to attract investment into it with the help of PPP.

Here are basic mechanisms of PPP used in international practice:[53]

- BOT (Build, Operate, Transfer). This mechanism is used mainly in concessions. Infrastructure object is created by the concessionaire, who, after the completion of construction, obtains the right to operate the constructed facility for a period that is sufficient for the return of the investment. Upon expiration, the object is returned to the state. The concessionaire receives the right to use, but not to own, the facility, which is owned by the state.
- BOOT (Build, Own, Operate, Transfer). In this case, the private party receives not only the right to use, but also to own the facility during the term of the agreement, after which it would transfer to the state. There is also the reverse BOOT, in which the state finances and constructs the infrastructure project, and then transmits it to the trust management of the private party, with the right of the latter to gradually repurchase it.
- BTO (Build, Transfer, Operate). This mechanism involves the transfer of the object to the state immediately upon completion of construction. After it is received by the state, it goes into use by the private party, but without the transfer of the ownership to the latter.
- BOO (Build, Own, Operate). In this case, the object created upon the expiration of the agreement is not transferred to the state and remains at the disposal of the investor.
- BOMT (Build, Operate, Maintain, Transfer). When using this mechanism, an emphasis is made on the responsibility of the private party for the repair and maintenance of the constructed infrastructure facilities.
- DBOOT (Design, Build, Own, Operate, Transfer). Agreements of this type are the responsibility of the private party not only for the construction of the infrastructure facility, but also for its design.

---

[53] http://www.veb.ru/common/upload/files/veb/ppp/actions/20091201/c0912_kabashkin1.pdf.

- DBFO (Design, Build, Finance, Operate). In this agreement, in addition to the responsibility for the design, the private party is responsible for the financing of the construction of infrastructure facilities.

The public–private partnership market in Russia is only beginning to take shape, so the study of foreign experience and the possibility of using its best examples can make a significant contribution to its formation.

## 6.2. PUBLIC–PRIVATE PARTNERSHIP IN THE REGIONS OF THE RUSSIAN FEDERATION

Currently Russia is implementing more than 200 PPP projects in the following areas: transportation, heating, water supply and sanitation, health and education, solid waste management, and science parks. As of November 2013 in 65 regions of the Russian Federation, regional laws have already been adopted on PPP; in 4 regions the laws are under consideration by the legislative bodies of the regions.[54]

The implementation of projects on the basis of PPP is distributed unevenly amongst regions. For example, among them are the pilot regions that have already achieved significant results in the PPP, regions where there are no implemented or implementable PPP projects, and regions that are just beginning to test this model on their territory.

Initially, the PPP projects were most widely used in the fields of transportation and public utility infrastructure. This largely can be explained by the depreciation of assets in these sectors of the economy. According to a famous Russian saying, one of the two main problems in Russia are roads, the repairs of which are expensive. The state cannot repair roads itself, especially if taking into account the heterogeneity of Russian regions; in certain regions, for example, there are roads that do not have a hard coating. The public utility infrastructure is in need of renovation and updating.

Therefore, the state predominantly encourages and initiates projects that are connected with the acute problems in these areas.

---

[54] Rating of Regions with PPP 2014. Development of public-private partnership in the Russian Federation. Moscow, Russia.: Center for the development of public-private partnership, 2014.

However, recently there has been a tendency for projects in the social sphere, related to the construction and reconstruction of schools, kindergartens, and hospitals. The Center for the Development of Public–Private Partnership[55] has published ratings of the regions for the development of PPP in the Russian Federation. The rating relies on the following criteria: the development of the institutional environment, the region's experience in the implementation of PPP projects, and investment attractiveness for the infrastructure investors. For example, among the 131 projects in the 60 regions, the social sphere is the absolute leader with 56 projects (including implemented, implementing, and future projects). There are 30 projects in the transportation sphere, 23 in the public sphere, and, notably, 22 projects in the energy sphere. The distribution among the federal districts is shown in the Table 6.1.[56]

**TABLE 6.1.**  The Comparison of Projects Implemented by Industry and by Federal Districts

| Federal District/ Industry | Public | Social | Transportation | Energy | Total |
|---|---|---|---|---|---|
| Far Eastern | - | - | 2 | 2 | 4 |
| Volga | 9 | 17 | 5 | 3 | 4 |
| Northwestern | 4 | 8 | 7 | 4 | 3 |
| North Caucasian | - | 3 | - | 1 | 4 |
| Siberian | 1 | 10 | 6 | 7 | 24 |
| Ural | 2 | 6 | 2 | 1 | 11 |
| Central | 5 | 7 | 5 | 4 | 21 |
| South | 2 | 5 | 3 | - | 10 |
| Total | 23 | 56 | 30 | 22 | 131 |

It is important to note that the first regions to start PPP projects are actively sharing their experiences, which allows others to travel the already "beaten path."

Authors classify regions by their level of PPP in the following ranks:

- Leading regions, whose experience can be considered as an example to the implementation of projects in other regions. This list includes: St. Petersburg, the Republic of Tatarstan, Novosibirsk Oblast, Nizhny Novgorod Oblast, Sverdlovsk Oblast, and Voronezh Oblast.

---

[55] http://pppcenter.ru/
[56] Rating of regions by PPP-2014. Development of public-private partnership in the Russian Federation. Moscow: Center for Public-Private Partnership, 2014.

It should be noted that St. Petersburg has become one of the pioneers among Russian regions to implement investment projects on the basis of PPP.

- Regions with high potential. These regions have little experience in the implementation of PPP projects (1–2 projects), high investment attractiveness, and emerging regulatory framework. Leaders in this category of classification are Moscow and Krasnodar Krai. It also includes: Perm Krai, Yaroslavl Oblast, Lipetsk Oblast, Samara Oblast, and the Khanty-Mansi Autonomous Okrug.
- Regions with average potential. These regions have conditions for PPP development and are testing PPP projects on their territory. These include: Moscow Oblast, Omsk Oblast, Kaliningrad Oblast, and Krasnoyarsk Krai.
- Regions with low potential. These are regions with a low level of development of legal framework and with low investment attractiveness. The authors emphasize that in this category only Murmansk Oblast and the Republic of Tuva have experience in implementing PPP projects.
- Regions with very low potential. These are the regions with the lowest scores in their experience with PPP projects (0 out of 10 points) and their level of investment attractiveness (1 out of 10 points). These include the Yamal-Nenets Autonomous Okrug, Kamchatka Krai, Zabaikalskii Krai, and other regions.

The total cost of PPP projects (including all stages of implementation) is 1.044 trillion rubles. The total amount of private investment in PPP projects is 913.4 billion rubles (87.44% of the total cost of the projects). There are 90 PPP projects that are currently under implementation and management.

In June 2008, on the basis of "Bank for Development and Foreign Economic Affairs (Vnesheconombank)," the State Corporation Center of Public–Private Partnership was established. Since 2012, the Directorate has been in operation with the mission of supporting and accelerating the development of infrastructure projects of national, regional, and local importance, as well as improving the quality of services that state and municipal governments provide to the development of infrastructure through the use of various tools of public–private partnership.[57]

To date, the Directorate contributes to the development of PPP by:

1. Providing investment advisory services on the implementation of development projects. Government of the Russian Federation Act of 17.08.2010 No 1372-r defined Vnesheconombank to be the only executor of investment consulting services for state use of Russian Federation subjects on the implementation of investment projects carried out in public–private partnership. Investment consultation was carried out during the construction of kindergartens in the Astrakhan Oblast, in the construction of a bridge complex in the Nizhny Novgorod Oblast, etc.

2. Implementing a financial program, adopted by the Supervisory Board of Vneshekonombank in 2010, that helps regional and urban development projects, and that is oriented to aid state and municipal authorities in their preparation of investment projects that address regional and urban development under the terms of public–private partnership.[58]

3. Creating education programs on the development and implementation of PPP projects and the retraining of state and municipal authorities, as well as other participants of the PPP market. That is why, in 2010, the Financial University of the Government of the Russian Federation together with Vnesheconombank created the "Public–Private Partnership" faculty. In 2012, there were more than 250 people who studied there as part of the training program, including representatives of other CIS countries. In February 2013, the first offsite training for representatives of state and municipal authorities of the Republic of Bashkortostan took place.[59]

4. Participating in the development of the area of Russian legislature that regulates relations arising in the organization of PPP projects, including the development of existing models and creation of new models of PPP. In particular, the drafting of the federal law "On the

[57] http://www.veb.ru/strategy/PPP/pppmission/
[58] http://pppinrussia.ru/main/metodicheskie_materiali/organizatsiya_proekta_gchp/finansirovanie_sodeistviya_proektam_razvitiya
[59] http://www.veb.ru/strategy/edu/cafedra_PPP/

basis of public–private partnership in the Russian Federation" is underway; proposals for improving the federal law "On Concession Agreements" were developed, etc. Particular importance should be given to the development, in accordance with Russian legislation and requirements, of the model of public–private partnerships referred to as "Build-Own-Lease-Transfer (BOLT)" – an analog to a widespread model in the West.

5.    Participating in dialog with international centers of PPP on questions of cooperation and promotion of the development of PPP in Russia and CIS countries.

As noted earlier, presently there are regions that have experience with PPP projects, which may be useful in the implementation of PPP development policy in other regions that are taking their first steps in this direction.

## 6.3. STRATEGIC SUCCESS FACTORS AND DIFFICULTIES IN IMPLEMENTING PPP PROJECTS ON THE REGIONAL LEVEL

The analysis of the current PPP industry situation in Russia allows the discovery of "success factors" in the implementation of PPP projects on the regional level, as well as difficulties in their development.

However, despite the fact that there are positive tendencies in the development of PPP in Russia, there are certain "stumbling blocks" that limit its effectiveness. The global practice defines these "blocks" as follows:[60]

- Mismatch between expectations and outcomes of partnership from both state and business;
- Lack of clear objectives and commitment to partnership from the state;
- Complex decision-making process;
- Vague state policy towards certain sectors of the economy;
- Lack of legal framework;
- Weak risk-management;

---

[60] Development barriers of PPP in Russia. M.; NPF "Expert Institute", 2010.

- Low trust in state policy;
- Insufficient development of local funds markets;
- Insufficient number of tools and mechanisms that attract long-term financial resources at reasonable prices – often the cost of private money is higher than public resources, which leads to a higher cost for the project;
- Low level of project transparency;
- Low level of competition due to the high cost of participation in tenders (call for bids) that leads to the increased costs of projects.

Undoubtedly the barriers listed above are present in Russian practice; however, given the fact that, in Russia, PPP is only beginning to develop, the question of obstacles in the implementation of PPP projects should be given particular attention so that it will be possible to subject it to a deeper analysis.

For a better understanding of the PPP market and a realistic assessment of the current situation, the participants, and firstly the private sector, which as a rule is the executor of projects, should be addressed.

## 6.4. STRATEGIC MANAGEMENT FORMS AND INSTRUMENTS FOR THE IMPLEMENTATION OF PROJECTS UNDER THE PUBLIC–PRIVATE PARTNERSHIP IN RUSSIA

### 6.4.1. INVESTMENT FUND PROJECTS

It is assumed that the state would finance business projects whose cost is no less then 5 billion rubles for the period of five years. The private investor would have to invest a minimum of 25% of the total cost. The profitability of the project should be no less then 4% and no more than 11%.

State support using the Investment Fund is conducted in three ways:

- Direct financing of the project;
- The participation of the shares and funds of the company that would be working on the project;

- The system of state guaranties that would be different from the current guarantees provided by the Ministry of Finance of the Russian Federation (since they do not need to be registered annually in the budget, and these funds are not considered to be "burnt" during the year).

There are two criteria that are used in the selection of projects: quality and quantity. National priority is specifically one of the quality criteria.

The quantity criteria consist of:

- overall economic efficiency, which is expressed in the project's contribution to regional growth and to gross domestic product;
- efficiency of a budget (growth of tax revenue); and
- financial performance (internal rate of return, index return on investment, and its time period).

The quantity criteria are approved by a joint order of both the Ministry of Economic Development and the Ministry of Finance of the Russian Federation.

## 6.4.2. CONCESSION PROJECTS

The state, as the full owner of the property, authorizes its private partner to perform within a certain period of time the agreed functions and provides him with the corresponding authority.

The concession implies that the grantor (the state) passes to the concessionaire the right to exploit natural resources, infrastructure, enterprises, and equipment. In return, the state receives compensation in the form of one-time (lump sum) or periodic (royalty) payments. Concession agreements are implemented on the basis of public property, including the use of state budget funds. In the absence of public property resources in the partnership, the private partner receives the right to conduct certain business—the exclusive right to conduct business that belongs to public law entities, for example, maintenance of parking lot activity, etc.

Primarily, the objects of the concession agreement are socially important objects that cannot be privatized. These include airports, railways, housing facilities and other infrastructure, as well as public transport systems, health, education, and culture and sports facilities.

## 6.4.3. RENT AND LEASING

The rent agreements underline that the state or municipal property is transferred to a private partner for temporary use for a fee. In these agreements, the mandatory rule is that the object of the lease is returnable, and the rights to dispose of the property are retained by the state and are not transferred to the private partner.

## 6.4.4. PRODUCTION SHARING AGREEMENT

This is the agreement under which the state provides entrepreneurs, on a reimbursable basis and for a fixed term, exclusive rights to explore and extract mineral resources on the subsoil indicated in the agreement, as well as the right to engage in a related work. The investor undertakes to conduct this work at his own expense and risk. In contrast to the concession, the private investor does not own the entire product output, but only the part of output that is stipulated by conditions of the contract. As a rule, parties involved in the production of petroleum products make such agreements.

## 6.4.5. STATE CONTRACTS

State contracts are completed by a client on behalf of the Russian Federation in order to insure public needs. The purpose of these contracts is the procurement of goods (works, services) for state or municipal needs, including in the state reserve.

## 6.4.6. INFRASTRUCTURE BONDS

Bonds are issued to finance the construction, acquisition, or renovation of infrastructure. The issuer of such bonds is a legal entity that implements infrastructure projects, including projects on the basis of a concession agreement. Creditors receive their payments on bonds from the operation of the infrastructure.

## 6.4.7. CONTRACT LIFE CYCLE (LCC)

Contract life cycle is a form of public–private partnerships that is used in foreign countries. The term "contract life cycle" is a translation of the term "Life Cycle Contract" used in the Nordic countries. In some European countries, the contract is called DBFM (Design-Build-Finance-Maintain) and is a form of concessions. In France, such contracts are called "partnership contracts."

Contract life cycle can be defined as a contract form of PPP, according to which the state partner on a competitive basis concluded an agreement with a private partner for the design, construction, and operation of the object for the period of the life cycle of that object. Payment on the project is made in equal shares after the commissioning of the object on the condition that the private partner maintains the facility in accordance with specified requirements.

The difference of LCC from other mechanisms for the implementation of PPP, applicable in Russia, consists of the following:

- The given contract includes all three life stages of the object – design, construction and operation;
- The private partner in the LCC is solely making decisions on all design and technical solutions that are needed for the implementation of the projects. The private partner is also liable for all technical hazards and design risks;
- Initially, the fundraising for the project is implemented by the private partner on the basis of a special project company;
- The state partner makes payments on the project only from the beginning of the object's operations;
- Payment for the project is an annual (or quarterly) "fee for service" and depends only on the completion of functional requirements that are in the contract. In the case of their incompletion, the special project company is subjected to penalties specified in the contract;
- The LCC contract does not include operation questions, e.g., the collection of payments for the usage of the infrastructure object. The payments for the service that were done by the state are only tied to the quality of the object;

- Ownership rights of the infrastructure facility may occur not only in the public, but also in the private party – depending on the project's specifics;
- Payments for service from the state partner should be guaranteed for the entire period of a contract.

## 6.5. STRATEGIC OBSERVATIONS

1. The interaction between private and public sector is weakly developed and inefficient.
2. There is a lack of unified methodology for the implementation of PPP projects.
3. The consolidation of the business community in the PPP field is needed.
4. The standardization of professional activities in the PPP field is premature, due to the fragmented nature of projects.
5. The state customers need to increase the level of special competences in the PPP field.
6. The business community lacks the exchange of experience with foreign partners.
7. The information about the development and trends of PPP projects in Russia is insufficient.

These findings may be useful in the development of recommendations to help improve the "climate" of PPP in the Russian regions.

# BIBLIOGRAPHY

Legal Acts:

1. "Strategy of socio-economic development of the Far East and the Baikal region for the period through 2025" approved by Instruction of the Government of the Russian Federation N2094-p. Dated 28.12.2009.
2. "Implementation of the federal target program 'Economic and social development of the Far East and the Baikal region for the period through 2018'" approved by Instruction of the Government of the Russian Federation N480. Dated 15.04.1996.
3. "Strategy of socio-economic development of Sakhalin Oblast for the period through 2025" approved by Instruction of the Government of Sakhalin Oblast N99. Dated 28.03.2011.
4. "On Amending the Instruction of the Government of the Sakhalin Oblast N99 from 28.03.2011 – "Socio-economic development strategy of Sakhalin Oblast for the period through 2025" approved by Instruction of the Government of Sakhalin Oblast N10. Dated 15.01.2014.
5. "Socio-economic development of Kuril Islands (Sakhalin Oblast) for the period from 2007 through 2015" target program approved by Instruction of the Government of the Russian Federation N478. Dated 09.08.2006.
6. "Economic development and innovation policy of Sakhalin Oblast for the period from 2014 through 2020" state program approved by Instruction of the Government of Sakhalin Oblast N352. Dated 12.06.2013.
7. "Industrial development in Sakhalin Oblast for the period through 2020" state program approved by Instruction of the Government of Sakhalin Oblast N808. Dated 31.12.2013.
8. "Development of the transport infrastructure and road facilities of Sakhalin Oblast for the period from 2014 through 2020" state

program approved by Instruction of the Government of Sakhalin Oblast N426. Dated 06.08.2013.

Main Research Publications:

1.  Ansoff, I. *Strategic Management*. London: Palgrave MacMillan, 2007.
2.  Badman, M. K., Guzner, S. S., Seliverstov, V. E. *Federal Assistance to Depressive and Falling Behind Regions in Russia*. Novosibirsk: EKOR, 1996.
3.  Chichkanov, V. P. *Principles and Methods of the Region's Long-term Economic Planning*. Moscow: The Science, 1986.
4.  Granberg, A. G. *Regional Economy Basics*. Moscow: HSE, 2000.
5.  Ignatova, T.V. *Economic Development: Regional Strategies and Technologies*. Rostov-on-Don: SKAGS, 1999.
6.  Kleshov, V. V., Badman, M. K. *The Territorial Production Complexes*. Nizhnee Priangariye. Novosibirsk: The Science, 1992.
7.  Kvint, V. L. *The Global Emerging Market: Strategic Management and Economics*. New York, London: Routledge, 2009.
8.  Kvint, V. L. *Strategy for the Global Market: Theory and Practical Applications*. New York, London: Routledge, 2016.
9.  Maskin, E., Dasgupta, P. (2005). "Uncertainty and Hyperbolic Discounting." *American Economic Review*, vol.9, no.4, pp. 1290–1299.
10. Mikheeva, N. N., Leonov, S. N. *Regional Economy and Management: Education Methodology Guideline*. Khabarovsk: PNU, 2000.
11. Parshev, A. P. *Why Russia is Not America*. Moscow: AST, Astrel, 2006.
12. Phelps, E. S. *Mass Flourishing: How Grassroots Innovation Created Jobs, Challenge, and Change*. Princeton: Princeton University Press, 2013.
13. Porter, M. E. "The Competitive Advantage of Nations." *Harvard Business Review*, March-April 1990.

# APPENDIX

The chart in this appendix shows the profitability of goods, products, and services sold in the Russian Far East, and the profitability of each organization's assets by economic activity, in percentages.[61]

---

[61] http://www.nalog.ru/rn77/taxation/reference_work/conception_vnp/

| | 2011 | | 2012 | | 2013 | |
|---|---|---|---|---|---|---|
| | Profitability of goods, products sold (work, services), %* | Profitability of assets, %** | Profitability of goods, products sold (work, services), %* | Profitability of assets, %** | Profitability of goods, products sold (work, services), %* | Profitability of assets, %** |
| Total | 11.5 | 7.0 | 9.7 | 6.8 | 7.7 | 5.0 |
| Agriculture, Hunting and Forest industries | 10.3 | 4.2 | 11.7 | 4.8 | 6.3 | 2.5 |
| Fishing Industry | 22.0 | 13.8 | 21.4 | 18.7 | 21.5 | 15.1 |
| Mineral Production, including: | 35.7 | 18.4 | 31.0 | 15.3 | 25.1 | 12.7 |
| energy producing minerals | 32.1 | 17.9 | 28.8 | 15.2 | 24.1 | 13.1 |
| other, non energy producing minerals | 64.5 | 20.6 | 48.2 | 16.0 | 33.2 | 10.3 |
| Processing industry, including: | 13.2 | 8.2 | 11.0 | 8.1 | 9.5 | 4.9 |
| Food production, including beverages and tobacco | 8.1 | 5.3 | 11.1 | 6.8 | 10.1 | 6.1 |
| Textile and clothing industry | 7.1 | 3.8 | 12.3 | 5.0 | 7.1 | 3.5 |
| Leather industry, footwear industry | 7.5 | 3.4 | 8.1 | 3.9 | 6.2 | 1.8 |
| Forest industry, wood products manufacturing | 5.9 | — | 5.3 | 2.1 | 8.1 | 1.8 |

| | 2011 | | 2012 | | 2013 | |
|---|---|---|---|---|---|---|
| | Profitability of goods, products sold (work, services), %* | Profitability of assets, %** | Profitability of goods, products sold (work, services), %* | Profitability of assets, %** | Profitability of goods, products sold (work, services), %* | Profitability of assets, %** |
| Paper industry; publishing and printing industry | 12.2 | 6.9 | 10.5 | 6.7 | 9 | 3.7 |
| Oil products industry; Coke production | 19.3 | 13.4 | 11.3 | 12.7 | 9.6 | 6.0 |
| Chemical industry | 24.8 | 17.1 | 22.9 | 15.8 | 16.7 | 7.5 |
| Rubber and Plastic industry | 7.2 | 6.0 | 9.1 | 8.3 | 8.7 | 6.0 |
| Other, non metal minerals production | 11.8 | 5.1 | 12.4 | 6.5 | 9.8 | 3.6 |
| Steel and finished metal goods production | 15.9 | 8.9 | 11.8 | 7.8 | 9.9 | 4.9 |
| Steel and finished metal goods production, including steel production | 17.6 | 9.5 | 12.6 | 8.1 | 10.3 | 5.0 |
| Finished metal goods production | 6.4 | 4.4 | 7.6 | 5.0 | 8.2 | 4.3 |
| Machinery and equipment production | 7.0 | 3.9 | 7.7 | 4.5 | 7.5 | 3.5 |
| Electrical and optic equipment production | 10.0 | 6.8 | 8.1 | 6.0 | 8.9 | 5.6 |
| Transportation machinery and equipment industry | 7.5 | 2.9 | 6.0 | 2.7 | 5.8 | 2.3 |

| | 2011 | | 2012 | | 2013 | |
|---|---|---|---|---|---|---|
| | Profitability of goods, products sold (work, services), %* | Profitability of assets, %** | Profitability of goods, products sold (work, services), %* | Profitability of assets, %** | Profitability of goods, products sold (work, services), %* | Profitability of assets, %** |
| Electric energy, gas and water production | 6.6 | 1.4 | 4.7 | 2.0 | 4.7 | 1.3 |
| Construction industry | 6.8 | 2.6 | 6.7 | 2.7 | 4.8 | 1.8 |
| Wholesale and retail trade; motor vehicles, household items and personal items repair, including: | 10.5 | 10.2 | 8.2 | 7.9 | 7.1 | 7.2 |
| Motor vehicles and motorbikes trade, repair and maintenance | 4.7 | 9.3 | 4.1 | 10.2 | 3.3 | 7.7 |
| Wholesale trade, including agents based trade, excluding motor vehicles and motorbikes trade | 13.8 | 10.8 | 10.5 | 7.8 | 9.4 | 7.4 |
| Retail trade, excluding motor vehicles and motorbikes trade; household items and personal items repair | 3.0 | 5.7 | 3.6 | 7.0 | 2.1 | 6.3 |

| | 2011 | | 2012 | | 2013 | |
|---|---|---|---|---|---|---|
| | Profitability of goods, products sold (work, services), %* | Profitability of assets, %** | Profitability of goods, products sold (work, services), %* | Profitability of assets, %** | Profitability of goods, products sold (work, services), %* | Profitability of assets, %** |
| Hotels and restaurants | 6.9 | 5.1 | 8.4 | 5.6 | 6.7 | 4.2 |
| Transportation and communication | 12.8 | 4.7 | 12.2 | 5.7 | 9.9 | 4.1 |
| Including communication | 24.6 | 9.0 | 26.7 | 8.3 | 26 | 8.4 |
| Finance industry | 0.0 | — | 0.4 | 4.5 | 0.4 | 5.7 |
| Real-estate industry rent and services. Including: | 10.4 | 1.4 | 10.0 | 2.5 | 9 | 0.1 |
| Scientific research and development | 10.7 | 2.5 | 8.8 | 2.4 | 7.8 | 2.2 |
| Government management and military defense; mandatory social security | 5.8 | 1.8 | 6.6 | 1.3 | 9 | 1.8 |
| Education | 5.5 | 3.9 | 7.2 | 5.1 | 5.3 | 4.1 |
| Health Care | 5.3 | 3.6 | 6.5 | 3.5 | 5.9 | 2.9 |
| Other social, public and personal services | 0.7 | 5.7 | — | 6.0 | — | 5.1 |

# INDEX